TRAVEL, TOURISM, AND HOSPITALITY LAW

SECOND EDITION

TRAVEL, TOURISM, AND HOSPITALITY LAW

SECOND EDITION

Alexander Anolik, Esq.

693 Sutter Street, Sixth Floor
San Francisco, California 94102
Telephone: (415) 673-3333
Fax: (415) 673-3548

Design and production: Backspace Ink

ISBN: 0-935920-60-9
Printed in the United States of America

ABOUT THE AUTHOR

Alexander Anolik, a San Francisco-based travel lawyer, author, and educator, is one of the foremost authorities on travel law.

He received his Juris Doctor degree from the University of California in 1967. He did graduate work in international law at the University of California and at the Academy of International Law, The Hague, Netherlands.

Mr. Anolik is a cofounder and president of the International Forum of Travel and Tourism Advocates (IFTTA) and vice chairman of the International Bar Association's Travel and Tourism Committee. Upon the endorsement of the United States government, he was selected as an associate member of The World Tourism Organization (WTO) of the United Nations.

He has taught travel law at Golden Gate University in San Francisco, Cañada College, the University of Hawaii and Cornell University, and has conducted numerous legal seminars for ICTA (the Institute of Certified Travel Agents), ASTA (the American Society of Travel Agents), and ARTA (the Association of Retail Travel Agents) whom he now serves as general counsel.

Mr. Anolik has been a legal consultant to numerous travel industry trade associations, airlines, cruise lines, government tourist offices, tour operators, and thousands of travel agents.

Mr. Anolik has served as legal editor and travel law columnist for numerous trade publications. He is a frequent contributor to many American and international travel and tourism periodicals. The author's dedication to conducting travel law training for industry students, as well as agents, has produced a wealth of Preventive Legal Care® training tapes, training textbooks, and articles. *Travel, Tourism, and Hospitality Law* has been designed to provide students, as well as those working in the industry, with the basic knowledge of travel law that must be studied and practiced to prevent legal problems.

The author wishes to thank the many international travel leaders and government officials participating in the University of Hawaii's EDIC program from the South Pacific and Asian Rim countries that annually contribute to this text and to their country's travel law infrastructure.

CONTENTS

INTRODUCTION

Ever since the United States government deregulated the travel industry in 1984, travel law, like society itself, has undergone tremendous changes. Certain basic legal concepts and theories remain as constants. Others keep changing to meet the needs of the travel industry, as well as the needs of consumers, and to adapt to changing international and domestic laws evolving around the travel industry. Preventive Legal Care® is a method of doing business for those working in the travel industry. It teaches both about the legal problems that may arise and how to avoid them. Preventive Legal Care® also provides the information needed for a strong defense should any claims be made against those working in the travel profession.

The purpose of this text is to bring the basics of travel, tourism, and hospitality law to all those working in the various segments of the travel industry, and to remind them of their legal rights, as well as their responsibilities. This book is *not* intended to replace the services of a travel lawyer. It is designed to help you do business in the travel industry, as well as in the business world. Knowledge of these basic concepts of travel law will help prevent future costly legal problems, or at least lessen damages in situations where legal complications arise.

Travel law is a relatively new area to the legal profession. It is amazing that there are not more trial attorneys, business attorneys, and legal scholars emphasizing or specializing in this industry, which is the number one or two service industry in most states and numerous countries. A variety of areas of travel law have been chosen to give you a broad understanding of the legal problems that can arise. We hope this information will help you understand the basic legal "buzz" words and theories that you will come across in the travel business and help protect you and your company from unnecessary legal complications. This text has been designed to be used in many of the vocational travel industry public and private travel training courses for a more complete training program to teach our industry the need to practice Preventive Legal Care®.

Tourism and travel law has recently been added as a specialized category within the Business Law section of the International Bar Association. Travel and tourism law is also the focus of the International Forum of Travel and Tourism Advocates (IFTTA), whose library was assembled from around the world. IFTTA has preserved books, articles, travel laws, regulations, case precedents, consumer disclosure notices and government directives to assist those interested in achieving a better understanding of travel laws within the travel, tourism, and hospitality communities.

This text will help students, academicians, and businesspeople to plan their legal strategies as conscientiously as they plan their business strategies. Only through a total understanding of the travel, tourism, and hospital industry, and the legal principles that help guide it, will there be fewer problems, fewer disappointments, and mutual respect for each other's legal rights and obligations.

IFTTA welcomes copies of new travel industry regulations and case decisions to be an internal source of research material. Donors are listed with their summarized material in *IFTTA News*:

IFTTA
c/o Anolik Law Offices
693 Sutter Street
San Francisco, CA 94102
415/673-3333
415/673-3548 FAX

CHAPTER 1

THE LEGAL STATUS OF A RETAIL TRAVEL AGENT

The retail travel agent is the nucleus of the travel industry. Travel agents coordinate and make arrangements between travel and tourism suppliers and the consuming public. Since travel agents act on behalf of and represent other groups, entities, or persons, they are, in fact, true agents. *Agency* is a legal concept, and it is defined as a fiduciary relationship whereby one person, the *agent*, represents another, the *principal*, in dealings with third parties. The agent acts for and in place of the principal and owes fiduciary obligations to the principal. Consequently, an act performed by an agent within the scope of the authority binds the principal. A *fiduciary obligation* is one in which one party imposes a special confidence in another, and from which the law implies an obligation upon the one in whom the confidence is imposed, a reciprocal obligation to act in good faith and with regard for the other's interests. This relationship is governed by common law and statute and, as we will see, involves various legally implied duties and obligations.

An agency is generally established by an agreement between the agent and the principal. The agreement may be either written or oral. However, in certain situations, an agency contract may be implied from the conduct of the parties. An agreement between the agent and the principal is needed to create an agency relationship.

Although agents are normally compensated for their efforts, monetary reward or payment is not a requirement. Even in cases where there is no fee, the agent is still held to a standard of care. Since the agent has a relationship with the traveler, the tour operator, and the various suppliers, such as airlines and hotels, one of the most frequently asked questions in the travel industry is what principal do travel agents represent and on whose behalf are they serving as agent? Before this question can be answered, the total circumstances regarding the relationship of the traveler, the tour operator, and the various suppliers must be analyzed.

THE RETAIL TRAVEL AGENT'S RELATIONSHIP TO THE AIRLINES

Most of the retail travel agents in the United States represent scheduled air carriers. If an agent has been approved by the Airlines Reporting Corporation (ARC) or the International Airlines Travel Agent Network (IATAN) within the United States, or the International Air Transport Association (IATA) internationally, the agent has agreed by contract to represent the air carriers that are members of these trade associations. In such cases, this binding contract between travel agent and air carrier is the Passenger Sales Agency Agreement.

Under the terms of the agency agreement, the travel agent is paid a commission for the sale of all passenger air transportation. Different airlines negotiate different commission rates with agents, depending on yield, productivity, scheduling, and competition in the area.

While acting as agent for an airline under the agreement, the travel agent agrees to carry out certain duties, including the maintenance of an office for the sale of air transportation, the promotion of the services of the various air carriers in every reasonable way, and the payment to the carrier of all monies due for the sale of air transportation. In return, the carrier agrees to pay the travel agent a certain rate of commission.

When the agent collects money for ticket sales and retains it for delivery to the various air carriers, the relationship between the agent and the principal airline is said to be a fiduciary relationship. A *fiduciary* is a person to whom property is entrusted for the benefit of another. The passenger sales agreement utilized by ARC, IATAN and IATA maintains that the agent is a trustee of the money that is collected from the traveler on behalf of the air carrier for the sale of air transportation. The contracts contend that all monies collected by the agent, including commissions, are retained or held in trust by the agent as the property of the carrier. However, the courts have occasionally ignored this contractual language and determined that money held by travel agents "in trust" for the carriers, actually belonged to the agents.

For example, in *Burks-Law v. Schneider,*[1] a creditor obtained a judgment against a travel agency, and sought to "levy" upon the agency's bank account. The agency claimed that this account contained the proceeds from airline ticket sales, which, according to its ATC agreements, was held "in trust" for the airlines. In

---

1. *Burks-Law v. Schneider*, California-Santa Clara County Superior Court No. 564849 (1986).

other words, the travel agency contended that the money did not belong to the agency, but instead to the airlines, and therefore the creditor could not seize it. The court, however, held that, in reality, no actual trust had been created, since the agency had commingled its agency general funds with the proceeds of the airline ticket sales. The creditor was allowed to levy upon the agency's ARC account to satisfy the judgment.

Common law has also provided certain guidelines that travel agents must follow when they enter into an agency agreement with an air carrier. Generally the agent has the responsibility of using reasonable care, diligence, and skill when selling or promoting air transportation. The agent must give an accounting to the air carrier when requested. Moreover, the agent may be liable to the air carrier for breach of contract, negligence, or intentional acts or omissions which cause damage or loss to the air carrier.

An example of this liability would be if a travel agent misrepresented the service or scheduling offered by a particular air carrier. According to general agency law, acts of an agent, within the scope of the agency, bind the principal. The contract created by a customer, who purchases a travel service through a travel agent, is a contract between the travel supplier/principal (i.e., air carrier, cruise line) and the customer. Therefore, the passenger might sue and recover damages against an airline because the service or scheduling was not as it was represented to be by the airline's "agent."[2] Under the airline's appointment agreement with travel agents, the agents would be liable by contract to compensate the airline for any damages incurred by the airline as a result of the travel agent's negligent acts or statements

---

2. See *American Express Co. v. Teitel*, 464 N.Y.S. 2d 947, 951 (N.Y. City Civ. Ct. 1983) and *Rappa v. American Airlines, Inc.*, 386 N.Y.S. 2d 612, 613 (N.Y. City Civ. Ct. 1976).

made in connection with its carrier agency appointment.

The carrier also has certain duties and obligations to the agent. Normally, the carrier will agree to hold the agent harmless, or not liable, for any injuries or loss to a third party caused by any act or omission of the carrier. The result of this relationship and the respective duties and obligations of the principal and agent is that both parties are ultimately responsible only for their own negligent acts or omissions.

In sum, the travel agent almost always represents the providers of travel services as a legal "agent," that is, airlines, cruise lines, tour operators, hotels, and ground transportation companies whose services the travel agent sells.

Occasionally, the travel agent will also be deemed to be the agent of the customer, as well, thus owing "fiduciary" (significant legal) obligations to the customer. That situation arises when the customer and travel agent act with the understanding that the customer is not merely purchasing a requested ticket, but is relying on the travel agent's expertise, to counsel the customer concerning a travel purchase.[3] In that situation, the travel agent is legally held to a higher standard of duty to the passenger, than where the travel agent is functioning as a mere "ticket agent."

This concept is often important, when the customer believes that the supplier/principal (the airline, cruise line, tour operator, hotel, or ground operator) has breached its agreement with the customer by failing to deliver what the customer understood he or she was purchasing. General agency law in effect, in almost all jurisdictions in the United States, holds that a *disclosed agent of a disclosed principal is not liable for breach of contract or negligence by that principal.* Thus, if the customer books a hotel suite through a travel agent, and upon arriving finds that only a room is available, although the customer has paid for a suite, then the hotel has breached its contract with the customer. Frequently, the customer, upon returning home, claims that the travel agent is somehow responsible, merely because the customer paid money to the travel agent, and it is much easier to sue the travel agent "at home" than the hotel or operator out of the jurisdiction.

Travel agents, however, are not insurers of the traveler's expectations or safety.[4] The law, if properly applied by the court, holds that, if travel agents disclosed the *fact* that they were acting as agents, and also disclosed the *identity* of the principal, the travel agents are not individually liable for breach of contract by the principal. The customer, in this example, must sue the hotel (provided the hotel has not already refunded that part of the customer's payments for the upgraded accommodations).

---

3. See *Rookard v. Mexicoach*, 680 F. 2d 1257 [9th Cir. 1982].
4. See *McCollum v. Friendly Hills Travel Center*, 72 Cal. App. 3d 83 (1985); *Levine v. General Mills, Inc., dba Olson Travelworld*, 519 F. Supp. 332 (N.D. Ga. 1981).

Because the law does not hold a disclosed agent of a disclosed principal liable for any breach of contract, or other breach of legal duty by the principal, it is important for travel agents to tell their customers their role as agent for the principal/travel suppliers, and the identity of those suppliers. A good Preventive Legal Care® procedure is for travel agents to print such a "disclosure notice" on the reverse side of every invoice, itinerary, and ticket jacket, informing customers of these facts. If an agent attempts to act on his/her own behalf, the principal is called an "undisclosed principal."

The following is a sample consumer disclosure notice:

CONSUMER DISCLOSURE NOTICE
[Part of Contract of Service]

PLEASE READ THIS NOTICE. IT CONSTITUTES PART OF YOUR CONTRACT FOR TRAVEL-RELATED SERVICES. PLEASE CHECK YOUR DOCUMENTS WHEN YOU RECEIVE THEM. CALL THE TRAVEL AGENCY IF YOU HAVE ANY QUESTIONS. MOST DISCOUNT FARES INVOLVE RESTRICTIONS. CHANGING CARRIERS OR FLIGHTS COULD RESULT IN THE AIRLINE DEMANDING AN INCREASED FARE. CHECK WITH THE AIRLINE OR THE TRAVEL AGENCY BEFORE MAKING ANY CHANGES.

[NAME OF TRAVEL AGENCY] (hereinafter "Travel Agency") is acting as a mere agent for SUPPLIERS (identified on the accompanying documents) in selling travel-related services, or in accepting reservations or bookings for services that are not directly supplied by this Travel Agency (such as air and ground transportation, hotel accommodations, meals, tours, cruises, etc.). Travel Agency, therefore, shall not be responsible for breach of contract, failure to comply with any laws such as the Americans with Disabilities Act (ADA), or any intentional or negligent actions or omissions on the part of such suppliers, which result in any loss, damage, delay, inconvenience or injury to travelers or travelers' companions or group members. Unless the term "guaranteed" is specifically stated in writing on your tickets, invoice, or reservation itinerary, Travel Agency does not guarantee any of such suppliers' rates, bookings, reservations, connections, scheduling, or handling of baggage or other personal effects. Travel agent shall not be responsible for any injuries, damages, or losses caused to any traveler in connection with terrorist activities, social or labor unrest, mechanical or construction failures or difficulties, diseases, local laws, climatic conditions, abnormal conditions or developments, or any other actions, omissions, or conditions outside the travel agent's control. Traveler assumes complete and full responsibility for, and hereby releases the agent from, any duty of checking and verifying any and all passport, visa, vaccination, or other entry requirements of each destination, and all safety and security conditions of such destinations, during the length of the proposed travel. However, we specifically recommend that U.S. citizens traveling to Canada, Mexico or the Caribbean, do so with a valid U.S. passport. For information

> concerning possible dangers at international destinations, contact the Travel Advisory Section of the U.S. State Department, (202) 647-5225. For medical information, call the U.S. Centers for Disease Control (CDC), (404) 332-4559. By embarking upon his/her travel, the traveler voluntarily assumes all risks involved in such travel, whether expected or unexpected. Traveler is hereby warned of the above risks as well as possible travel industry bankruptcies and medical and climatic disruptions, and the possibility traveler may be unable to travel as scheduled because of personal emergency. Traveler is advised to obtain appropriate insurance coverage against these risks; information is available through this Travel Agency regarding travel insurance. Traveler's retention of tickets, reservations, or bookings after issuance shall constitute a consent to the above and an agreement on his/her part to convey the contents hereto to his/her travel companions or group members.
>
> *[This is a sample only, and is not intended as legal advice. Travel agencies contemplating use of this Disclaimer should tailor it to their own individual circumstances, and obtain the advice of their own counsel before using it.]*

If the activity of the travel planning is more adventurous, the following tour operator type of notice is more appropriate:

CONSUMER DISCLOSURE NOTICE FOR SPORTING/ADVENTURE TOURS

Release and Assumption of Risk

I understand and I am aware that during the trek, tour, expedition, or other trip or vacation in which I am now participating, or in which I will participate, under the arrangements of ________________ and its agents, employees, associates, affiliated companies, or subcontractors, certain risks and dangers may arise, including, but not limited to, the hazards of traveling in unsafe areas or under unsafe conditions, the hazards of traveling in politically unstable areas, the dangers of civil disturbances and war, the forces of nature, the negligent or reckless acts or omissions of ________________, its agents, employees, officers, directors, associates, affiliated companies, or subcontractors, travel by boat, automobile, train, ship, aircraft, or other means of conveyance, and accident or illness in remote places without access to medical facilities, transportation, or means of rapid evacuation and assistance. Travel agent shall not be responsible for any injuries, damages, or losses caused to any traveler in connection with terrorist activities, social or labor unrest, mechanical or construction failures or difficulties, diseases, local laws, climatic conditions, abnormal conditions or developments, or any other actions, omissions, or conditions outside the travel agent's control. Traveler assumes complete and full responsibility for, and hereby releases the agent from any duty of, checking and verifying any and all passport, visa, vaccination, or other entry requirements of each destination, and all safety or security conditions at such destinations, during length of the proposed travel.

In consideration of, and as a part of the payment for, the right to participate in such treks, tours, expeditions, or other activities and in consideration of, and as a part of the payment for, the services arranged for me by ________________and its agents, employees, associates, affiliated companies, or subcontractors, I have and do hereby expressly assume all of the above risks, including, to the extent permitted by law, the risk of negligent or reckless acts or omissions of _______________, its agents, employees, officers, directors, associates, affiliated companies, or subcontractors, and I do hereby expressly agree to hold___________________ and its agents, employees, officers, directors, associates, affiliated companies, and subcontractors harmless and defend them against any and all liability, actions, causes of action, debts, suits, claims, and demands of any and every kind and nature whatsoever which I now have or which may hereafter arise out of agents, employees, associates, affiliated companies, or subcontractors. The terms of this agreement shall serve as a release and express assumption of risk for myself, my heirs, assignees, administrators, executors, and all members of my family, including any minors accompanying me. I have read and fully understand the provisions and the legal consequences of this Release and Assumption of Risk, and I hereby agree to all of its conditions, especially noting and agreeing to the portion of this provision that releases ____________ and its agents,

> employees, officers, directors, associates, affiliated companies, and subcontractors, to the extent permitted by law, from liability for the negligent or reckless acts or omissions of __________________ , its agents, employees, officers, directors, associates, affiliated companies, and subcontractors.
>
> *In calculating the cost of the tour or trip, __________________ has relied on travelers' consent to the terms and on their enforceability. In the absence of this release, the tour/trip cost would have been higher.*
>
> [To be printed on invoice, computerized itinerary, or travel documents.]

With consumers becoming increasingly litigious, every travel agency should consider purchasing errors and omissions ("E&O") insurance. This insurance covers the travel agency for any acts of negligence in performing services as a travel agent. If a travel agency finds itself named as a defendant in a lawsuit arising out of its provision of travel agency services, the agency can merely forward the suit to its E&O insurer, and that insurer will be obligated to *tender* a legal defense to the lawsuit (hire and pay for lawyers to defend the travel agency), and, if liability is found, pay the judgment (up to the policy limits).

Further, travel insurance is widely available to travelers. It is a wise Preventive Legal Care® measure for travel agencies to have brochures or other information handy for all customers describing the availability of travel insurance. Commonly, travel insurance provides coverage for (1) lost baggage and personal possessions; (2) medical expenses—including accidents while traveling; (3) trip cancellation or trip interruption; and (4) flight insurance for accidental death or injury during an air flight or cruise (lump sum payment). Particularly helpful to the travel agent is the trip cancellation or trip interruption coverage, which provides insurance if the traveler cannot travel because of the bankruptcy or default of an airline, tour operator, or cruise line.

Travelers, having purchased insurance covering their trips, will look to their insurance company for recovery if the carrier or tour operator files for bankruptcy, or otherwise defaults, and not to the travel agency.

If an agent attempts to become an independent contractor, rather than an employee, his/her liability may become greater since he/she may have assumed more responsibility with independent activity.

RESEARCH AND REVIEW

1. Define the term "agency" and explain how it determines who might be responsible for problems experienced by travelers.
2. Can a carrier be held responsible for carrying passengers who bought tickets from an agent that failed to forward payment to the carrier?
3. Why would a travel agency wish to use a "disclosure notice" for its customers?
4. What obligations do travel agents owe their customers, and what obligations are not owed?
5. Describe how an agent can practice Preventive Legal Care® and shift risks and liability to the traveler.

NOTES

CHAPTER 2

COMPANY FORMATION

One of the most important decisions in operating a successful travel venture is deciding what type of legal ownership is best for your travel activities. There are several ways that a person can own or operate a business, including a corporation, a limited partnership, a full partnership, a sole proprietorship, or a joint venture. Each of these business structures has its own set of rules and legal characteristics. In order to make the most profit, the travel agent should look at all types of legal entities and examine their tax consequences and potential legal liabilities.

THE SOLE PROPRIETORSHIP

The sole proprietorship is perhaps the simplest way to operate a business. It is commonly found in the "mom and pop" type of travel agency, which is owned and operated by a husband and wife team. The simple structure of the agency gives direct management and control to the principal owners.

There are no formal procedures required for forming a sole proprietorship other than obtaining a basic business operating license or permit from the local or state government. If the agency is using a name other than the name of the principal owner, a fictitious business name statement must be filed with the county clerk in the county where the primary place of business is located. A Notice of a Fictitious Business Name Statement is then published in a local newspaper of general circulation in the county. Following publication for the statutory time period, a proof of publication is then filed with the county clerk's office.

One major advantage to the sole proprietorship is the cost of formation, which is lower than the cost of either a partnership or a corporation. Since the owners have total ownership and control of the agency, the business may be freely transferred without the worry of accounting to partners or shareholders.

Because the sole proprietorship is run rather informally, and is merely an extension of the principal owners, it is difficult to separate the owner's financial investment in the business from his or her own personal property. Therefore, the law places a greater burden upon the sole proprietor with respect to the owner's personal liability for business obligations. The owner risks having personal assets attached or levied upon, as a result of litigation against the agency. Thus, the major disadvantage of operating as a sole proprietorship is the great potential for personal liability and loss, should the agency be subject to a judgment.

With certain limitations, upon the death of the sole owner, the "good will" or expected continued patronage of the travel agency passes to the estate of the deceased owner. Both ARC and IATAN agreements provide that the executor or other personal representative of a decedent's estate may enter into a temporary agreement with ARC and IATAN in order to preserve the good will of the agency. Any transfer of the agency business to an heir or other person is deemed to be a "change of ownership," and standard ARC/IATAN procedures for change of ownership must be followed.

In view of the increasing number of lawsuits in the travel industry, most travel attorneys advise against operating as a sole proprietorship because of the potential for personal liability judgments being made against agencies so operated.

THE GENERAL PARTNERSHIP

The general partnership is a more formal type of organization than the sole proprietorship. A general partnership is usually created by a written agreement between two or more persons who desire to conduct business for profit as co-owners. The co-owners agree to share profits as well as losses. The agreement is referred to as the articles of partnership or the partnership agreement. Each state has rules and regulations that govern the operation of partnerships within their respective jurisdictions. There is also a Uniform Partnership Act, which has been either partially or completely adopted by most states.

The general partnership entity may obtain limited protection for its name by the filing and publishing of a Fictitious Business Name Statement. The entity should also record a statement of partnership in each county in which a partner owns real property or is doing business.

Unlike the hands-on operation of a sole proprietorship, monetary contributions in general partnerships must be handled more formally. Each partner is entitled to a strict accounting of income, expenditures, and disbursements by the partnership. Management and control are usually allocated according to the percentage of ownership interest of each partner. Moreover, each partner is entitled to an accounting of the partnership's business operations in order to prepare his or her individual income tax returns.

It has been said that a partnership is very much like a marriage. Each partner may bind the other partners to a contract or agreement together with the risk of liability for business obligations. Liability to outsiders, or third parties, is joint liability without limitation. Therefore, you should choose your partners very carefully.

Any time two or more persons own a travel agency, they all become general partners, and the agency is operated as a general partnership *unless* the partners comply with the specific legal procedures for operating as a "limited partnership."

Unlike the sole proprietorship, where ownership of the agency can be transferred freely, in general partnerships any attempted transfer of one partner's interests must be approved by the remaining partners.

In preparing an income tax return, a partner's share in the profits of the partnership is taxable to the individual partner. Although the partnership as an entity must file a partnership informational return, the income tax payable by each partner is individual income.

THE LIMITED PARTNERSHIP

A limited partnership is more formal than the general partnership. In such situations, there are a number of limited partners whose liability in the partnership is confined to their individual financial investment. The day-to-day business operations of the agency are controlled by one or more general partners. The general partner makes the business decisions for the partnership and bears full and unlimited responsibility for his

or her actions. There is no limit on the general partner's liability for the actions of the partnership.

While limited partners have no voice in the day-to-day management decisions of the partnership, they do have the advantage of having limited liability for any loss incurred by the partnership.

Limited partnership as a form of ownership is not generally recommended for smaller agencies. It is more effectively used to raise funds or to set up a special project for the larger travel syndications and wholesale tour operators. This is because the operators of the syndication seek to raise investment capital, without adding partners wanting control of the day-to-day operations of the business. By offering limited partnership" interests to investors, the general partners need not relinquish control of the business, and the limited partners, in exchange, are assured that their liability in connection with the business will be limited only to the amount of their investment. Each state has its own rules and regulations concerning the operation of limited partnerships. The silent partner who puts up the money to start an agency and only intends to obtain travel benefits and tax advantages, but not work in the agency, is a typical industry example of a limited partner.

THE CORPORATION

The corporate entity is a form of business operation that is strongly favored. The corporate entity is quite flexible and offers the added benefit of limited liability to the corporate shareholders. In short, the corporate entity offers the travel agency, tour operator, or agency manager the greatest amount of flexibility with the greatest amount of protection against liabilities for business obligations.

A corporation is an entity that is legally recognized as a separate "person" under the law. However, to obtain the protections offered by the corporate entity, the laws of corporate formation must be strictly followed. Although the filing costs of forming a corporation are considerably higher than forming a sole proprietorship or a partnership, the added protections more than justify the increased costs. From the standpoint of legal fees, there may not be much difference.

In most jurisdictions, the corporate name is entitled to statewide protection under the laws of the state in which it is incorporated. The business name of the incorporated travel agency is thus protected on a statewide basis through the filing of the articles of incorporation, which should justify the corporate filing fees. Through federal trademark registration or registration with the various states, a corporation may obtain nationwide protection for its name.

According to law, the travel agency as a corporation is separate and distinct from the persons who own and manage the agency. When dealing with a corporate entity, one must separate the various groups of individuals involved with the corporation, including the corporate entity, the shareholders, the officers and directors, and the corporate employees.

Since the corporation is a separate legal entity, it has a legal capacity to enter into contracts in its own name, to sue or be sued, and to own or convey property. Fortunately, it takes no vacations and is always on time.

The shareholders of the corporation are the owners of the corporation. The shareholders as owners do not share in the direct management or control of a corporation. Shareholders elect the directors of the corporation and are entitled to receive the profits made by the corporation. The board of directors will determine the distribution of profits, and such distribution is referred to as dividends.

The board of directors elects the officers of the corporation. The officers are responsible for executing the day-to-day managerial functions of the corporation based on the policies and decisions laid down by the board of directors. While the directors are not considered employees of the corporation, the corporate officers are indeed corporate employees. Therefore, in addition to the advantages of a separate legal entity with limited liability for the owners, a corporation offers centralized management to control the general affairs of the business operation.

Other advantages to forming a corporation are the perpetual existence of the corporate entity and the free transfer of shares.

It must be noted, however, that the protections and advantages of the corporate entity will be lost if all of the corporate formalities are not followed. Under a legal theory known as "alter ego," the owners of a corporation may be held personally liable for obligations of the corporation where the evidence shows that the corporate entity was a sham extension of the individual owners. The courts usually look to see whether the required corporate meetings were held, whether proper articles of incorporation were filed, whether the funds of the owners were commingled with corporate funds, or whether the corporation was undercapitalized for the type of business in which it was engaged.

RESEARCH AND REVIEW

1. Describe the prerequisites for forming a corporation in your state.
2. List the advantages of becoming a corporation for a travel agency.
3. List the disadvantages to incorporate for a travel agency.
4. Describe two types of partnerships and list their advantages and disadvantages for travel agencies.

CHAPTER 3

CO-OPS, CONSORTIUMS, AND FRANCHISE ARRANGEMENTS IN THE TRAVEL INDUSTRY

Recent trends in the travel industry have led to the formation and development of large-scale travel agent cooperatives and consortiums. These new business structures have introduced many economic efficiencies to the operation of retail travel agencies.

COOPERATIVES

A cooperative, or "co-op," as it is frequently called, is, according to Webster's, "an enterprise or organization owned by and operated for the benefit of those using its services."

Volume purchasing power

Through their sheer purchasing power, co-ops, like consortiums and franchises, are frequently able to negotiate higher commissions and other favorable terms with so-called "preferred" suppliers. Suppliers are willing to offer these concessions because they are able to increase their volume through sales to co-op members. Some co-ops have established payment protection plans for member/customers booking preferred suppliers. This gives the customer an incentive to book the preferred supplier by offering the customer something in return—essentially, "insurance" against a default by a co-op preferred tour operator or other supplier.

CONSORTIUMS

A consortium is customarily a nonmember-owned business association whose purpose is to provide services to its members.

Like a cooperative, a consortium takes advantage of economies of scale in the travel industry through volume purchasing. A consortium will often negotiate override commissions and other favorable terms with "preferred" suppliers. Frequently, the consortium will offer its members a 24-hour emergency reservation service and discounted hotel chain and car rental rates. The objective and advantage of co-op or consortium membership is that, through "volume purchasing," it allows a small- to medium-sized travel agency achieve the same economies of scale enjoyed by the largest travel agencies. These smaller agencies, therefore, are able to compete in these areas with the larger travel agencies.

The United States Supreme Court delivered an indirect "shot in the arm" to co-ops and consortiums in the travel industry in its decision in the matter of *Northwest Wholesale Stationers v. Pacific Stationery & Printing Co.*[1] This case involved a wholesale buying cooperative, whose members, office supply retailers, were prohibited through their bylaws from also selling wholesale. By joining together in the cooperative, members were able to achieve "economies of scale in purchasing and warehousing that would otherwise be unavailable to them."

Pacific Stationery sold at both wholesale and retail levels, and was summarily expelled from the cooperative. Pacific Stationery then sued the cooperative, alleging that the cooperative had committed a *per se* violation of the federal antitrust laws (Sherman Act). The U.S. Supreme Court refused to find the cooperative *per se* liable, and essentially ruled that wholesale buying cooperatives were good things for the economy and for competition, and that it would not apply a *per se* rule against a cooperative in this situation.

The court endorsed "wholesale buying cooperatives" from an antitrust perspective. The court stated:

---

1. *Northwest Wholesale Stationers v. Pacific Stationery & Printing Co.,* 105 S.Ct. 2613 (1985).

> *Wholesale purchasing cooperatives ... are not a form of concerted activity characteristically likely to result in predominantly anticompetitive effects. Rather, such cooperative arrangements would seem to be "designed to increase economic efficiency and render markets more, rather than less, competitive."*

The Supreme Court signaled to co-ops and consortiums that use of their bulk purchasing power to obtain discounted prices, increased commissions, and other favorable terms was a positive, rather than negative, phenomenon in terms of the United States antitrust laws.

It is important to recognize, however, that, while a consortium and its members may designate "preferred" suppliers, they must not "boycott" those suppliers who refuse to offer favorable terms to the consortium. Specific acts of competitors designed to force a supplier to do business with them on certain terms normally constitute antitrust violations. Initially, consortiums catered to agencies that were either leisure-vacation agencies or corporate-business agencies. The earlier consortiums concentrated on a limited number of preferred suppliers catering to different destinations. This will no doubt be modified in the future to follow the lead of the consortiums TIME (Travel Industry Marketing Enterprises) and GEM (Go Earn More), two of the leading leisure agency consortiums that entered into agreements with one of the leading corporate and cruise consortiums to utilize each other's benefits and suppliers for greater variety and bargaining power.

FRANCHISES

Franchising is a relatively new concept to the travel industry. One distinguishing aspect of a franchise arrangement is that the customers of the travel agency can identify the relationship between the franchise name and the travel agency itself, although often the precise relationship between a company-owned franchise and an independently owned and operated franchise is not easily recognized by the general public. Franchisees have the right to use the trademark and trade name of the franchisor. Some customers feel somewhat more at ease knowing that they are dealing with a company name known for its integrity.

While travel agent members of a cooperative or consortium retain their own identity as a distinct service and product entity, franchisors, as a rule, do not. A franchisor normally dictates to its travel agent franchisees many procedures and restrictions on how the agents may conduct their businesses. A franchisor has developed a marketing scheme which enables the agent to enter the market without the problems often associated with starting any small business. In addition, the franchisor may have professional consultants available to help the agent to compete in today's deregulated aviation marketplace. Without going into extensive detail in this chapter, you should know that many states have enacted extensive laws by which franchisors must register with the Secretary of State or the Department of Corporations, and, if necessary, a prospectus must be filed with the Federal Securities and Exchange Commission.

The early days of franchising in the travel industry were not glamorous. The companies that first sprouted up were unfamiliar with the many problems of organization, promotion, marketing, and sales generation capacity involved in starting a travel agency business. As a result, most of the early franchise networks have disappeared from the scene, leaving many small-scale, independent businesspersons unable to recover money spent on projects that, all too often, turned out badly. Millions of dollars were wasted because outsiders to the industry thought selling travel was like selling fast foods, and, prior to deregulation and rebating, the concept of joining together for marketing was premature for the travel industry.

Since the early bugs have been ironed out, franchising firms are competing to sign up agencies to operate under the banner of the agency franchise network. Their advertisements often emphasize that independent agents are unable to compete effectively due to deregulation.

Agents may receive such items as an exclusive sales territory that might violate antitrust laws if attempted by a co-op or consortium. Franchise benefits might include agency listings in the local Yellow Pages, free signs, inclusion in national consumer advertising programs, as well as national sales team support, training programs, and bonus programs for individual travel agents within the agency. In addition, profits may be increased through access to 24-hour, seven-day-a-week emergency assistance telephone numbers for the traveling consumer, networking (i.e., incentive travel conventions and trade shows), customized tour products, corporate sales kits, and corporate hotel directories.

Franchise agreements between franchisors and the agency contain various items, which at first glance seem to restrict the manner in which the agents may operate. Nevertheless, many agents do not seem to mind giving the franchise network an initial sum ranging anywhere from $15,000 to above $40,000 in order to obtain the benefits of being associated with a particular franchise. Many agreements contain, in part, the following items:

1. The agency shall be exclusively identified with the particular trade name or logo of the franchise;
2. The agent and its employees must attend mandatory training workshops;

3. The agent must maintain high professional and ethical standards;
4. The agent must maintain and keep such business records as the franchisor may dictate and allow inspection of the records for the benefit of the franchisor;
5. The agent must follow a confidential "procedures manual";
6. The agency must agree to pay the franchisor certain sums of money for an initial period based upon the volume of sales generated by the agency.

Lastly, while some agents feel that they have received their investment value plus more from affiliation, many other agents believe that their investment, in terms of money and labor, has not been justified because of the minimal return the new agency realized. Many agents have complained that the representations and warranties made by the franchise sales representative were not true, and had the facts been known, they would not have invested in the franchise. Litigation against the franchisor, unfortunately, has often followed.

While affiliation with a travel agency franchise may increase the visibility of your agency and give it a higher profile in the community, before investing in a franchise make sure that you have thoroughly reviewed the prospectus, have detailed knowledge of what the franchisor may give to you, and obtain as many representations as possible in writing. Always remember that it is up to the agency to stimulate and generate sales and marketing techniques on its own behalf. The franchisor cannot operate a travel agency business for you. To obtain ROI (Return on Investment), a prospective franchise should carefully calculate whether the payment of a $42,000 franchise fee plus monthly fees, compared to a $3,000 one-time consortium fee, will ever be paid back with a future of lower commissions being predicted.

Since franchising regulations are so technical, the administrative and legal costs to establish a network are usually prohibitive to most groups or individuals wanting to use their years of expertise to form their own franchise operation. In one major franchise attempt, which did not succeed even though owned by one of the world's major communications networks, the franchisor was alleged to have spent $150,000 in legal fees just for its *prospectus*—the legal offering that is given to possible franchisees. The key point to remember is that the legal requirements of franchising are very technical. You should not attempt variations of a franchise, such as selling your expertise and name, unless all requirements are met. If it walks like a duck and talks like a duck, it's going to be called a duck. If it sounds and works like a franchise, it's going to be called a franchise by the appropriate state regulatory agency.

RESEARCH AND REVIEW

1. What is a travel industry co-op?
2. What is a travel industry consortium?
3. What is a travel industry franchise?
4. Define a travel industry trade association (i.e., ARTA—Association of Retail Travel Agents; ASTA—American Society of Travel Agents).

CHAPTER 4

EMPLOYMENT RELATIONS

Many books are available on the subject of labor relations and labor laws. For the travel agent it is important to have a basic understanding of the general concepts concerning the relationship between employee and employer and their respective duties and obligations. In particular, an employer should have a clear understanding of the "dos and don'ts" of labor management. Other issues of importance to the labor manager include theories of recovery for wrongful discharge under state law, sexual harassment claims, maternity leave disputes, and employee health and safety issues. Most of these laws are designed to protect employees and are easily interpreted in their favor.

WRONGFUL DISCHARGE

Historically, many states have laws that recognize the concept that, unless there is a written agreement stating otherwise, an employment can be terminated at the will of either party upon due notice. In recent years, however, various courts have demonstrated a willingness to protect employees from arbitrary or unreasonable termination. As a general rule, an employer must now have a legitimate business reason for terminating an employee. Moreover, the employer must act reasonably and fairly in carrying out the discharge and termination.

Most employers do not use written employment contracts with their employees, and management must be careful to avoid any type of representation that would form the basis for a claim of implied contract. It is wise for an employer to develop an employee handbook or manual, such as the ARTA employment manual, that describes each position within the company and the expected duties and responsibilities of each employee. The employee manual should also clearly state the duration of any type of probationary period for the employee.

In the event an employee is discharged and then sues for wrongful dismissal, the court will look at various factors to determine whether compensation is appropriate under a theory of implied contract. The court will examine the duration of the employment, any praise, commendations, or promotions received by the employee, as well as the lack of criticism of the employee's work. Many states now recognize the theory that every employment contract, and indeed every contract, has a covenant of good faith and fair dealing implied within the contract. Under this theory, both the employee and the employer are bound by the implied promise that each will act in good faith when dealing with one another and will not terminate the employee/employer relationship without reasonable justification.

In reviewing the basis of a termination of an employee, the court is particularly concerned with certain categories that are highly suspect and subject to close scrutiny. It is well established that an employee cannot be dismissed simply because of national origin, religious or political belief, sex, sexual preference, or involvement with labor organizing activities. If an employer dismisses or terminates an employee for any of these reasons, and the employee is able to convince the court of this, the employer may have to pay punitive damages. In addition, an employer may be liable for punitive damages if the employee is terminated because of a refusal to participate in any illegal activity or to take actions that would run contrary to the state public policy.

Two recent case law examples prohibiting discharges as "contrary to public policy" were (1) a gasoline company employee discharged after he refused to participate in an illegal price-fixing scheme, and (2) a "whistle-blowing" employee discharged after reporting to health authorities of a grocery store's instruction to deliver spoiled milk.

Before an employee is terminated, the business manager must determine whether the employee's conduct justifies the termination of the contract. For example, the firing of an airline ticket agent was upheld because the agent was guilty of holding space for his family by making bogus airline reservations. Employers wanting to discharge employees should try and keep employee files documenting warnings and past problems.

SEXUAL HARASSMENT AT THE WORKPLACE

In recent years, there has been a more intense focus on the issue of sexual harassment at the workplace.

Although this is generally thought of as a woman's issue, in an employment context it applies to both sexes. Women are beginning to assert their rights and seek protection under Title VII of the Civil Rights Act of 1964.

Sexual harassment is defined to include "any unwelcome sexual advances, requests for sexual favors, and other verbal or physical conduct of a sexual nature when such conduct has the purpose or effect of unreasonably interfering with an individual's performance or creating an intimidating, hostile, or offensive working environment."

Under this definition, the offender cannot simply claim that no harm was intended. The actions can be punished if they have that result.

If the incidence of sexual harassment caused the employee to resign or quit the company to escape additional harassment, the employee may file a "constructive discharge" lawsuit at the same time as filing a sexual harassment suit. *Constructive discharge* means that, even though the employer didn't actually fire the employee, conditions were intentionally made so unpleasant for the employee that it amounted to a "constructive" firing. Thus, the employee alleges that the conditions created by the employer were tantamount to actual firing.

Travel managers should also be aware of a legal theory called *respondeat superior.* Under this theory, an employer may be responsible for the acts of supervisory employees as they relate to sexual harassment regardless of whether the employer knew or should have known of their occurrence. Since the supervisor is acting within the apparent scope of the authority entrusted to him or her by the employer, the employee is responsible for the supervisor's actions. In comparison, an employer is not liable for the acts of harassment by co-workers unless the employer knew or should have known of the existence of the conduct.

Employers can protect themselves by making specific reference in the firm's personnel manual, and also in postings on employee bulletin boards, and other written materials relating to personnel practices, that sexual harassment of other employees is against the law and will be grounds for termination. Again, this is an example of the use of Preventive Legal Care® to avoid a legal problem from developing in the first instance.

HEALTH AND SAFETY ISSUES AT THE WORKPLACE

An employer must provide employees with a safe and reasonably healthy working environment. The individual states and local authorities monitor the workplace environment under the umbrella of their inherent police powers.

Two major health issues facing workers in today's travel industry are the extensive use of video display terminals (VDTs) and the rights of nonsmokers. Research into the effects of prolonged use of VDTs is still inconclusive, although the matter is being debated by medical experts. There have been claims by employees who use the terminals of pregnancy problems, eye strain, deteriorating vision, and lower back pain. It may be a good idea to provide rest breaks from the use of VDTs and to tell employees about preventive methods and exercises that minimize the potential health risks. If the travel agency staff is large enough, duties may be rotated among the various employees to minimize the actual amount of time each uses the VDT.

The question of smoking at the workplace has long been the subject of heated debate. Some local jurisdictions, most notably San Francisco, have passed ordinances regulating smoking at the workplace. While debate about the effects of second-hand smoke continues, for the moment the rights of nonsmokers to be totally without risk seem to be the prevailing view. When space allows, an employer may have separate rooms for smokers and nonsmokers or, if office space is limited, provide partitions, ventilation systems, and air purifiers. If the employer does not have enough space to accommodate both the smoker and the nonsmoker, then the nonsmokers have the right to a smoke-free working environment.

MATERNITY LEAVE DISPUTES

Under the pregnancy discrimination act amendment to Title VII of the Civil Rights Act, it is unlawful for an employer to discriminate among employees based upon pregnancy. The failure of an employer to pay pregnancy-related disability benefits, while paying benefits for other disabilities to other employees who are unable to work, is considered unlawful discrimination. Additionally, if the employer extends job reinstatement to employees after periods of temporary physical disability, the same policy must be followed when a woman chooses to begin working at the end of her pregnancy. If the business is using an employee manual, a clear program and policy for maternity leave should be developed and put in writing. The business manager should also recognize the implied theory of good faith and fair dealing in determining a maternity leave program for his or her employees.

AMERICANS WITH DISABILITIES ACT (ADA)

All U.S. businesses with 15 or more full- or part-time employees must comply with the Americans with Disabilities Act (ADA). That law requires employers NOT to discriminate in hiring or employment against any individual on the basis of physical or mental disability. Employers are required to make "reasonable accommodation" or any such disability. "Disability" is defined as "A physical or mental impairment that substantially limits one or more of the major life activities of such individual." Employers violating the ADA may be held liable for compensatory and punitive damages to the disabled individual, as well as for his or her attorney's fees and court costs, subject to certain limits depending upon how many individuals the employer has on the payroll.

RESEARCH AND REVIEW

1. List situations in which a travel agency can and cannot terminate an employee.
2. Why is it prudent for a travel agency to have an employee handbook or manual?
3. May a travel agency dismiss an employee if he/she attempts to unionize the agency?
4. Is an employer liable for sexual harassment by one of his/her employees by another? Explain.
5. Describe the current thinking on smokers' versus nonsmokers' rights in the workplace.

CHAPTER 5

CONTRACTS

You cannot exist in the business world without entering into some form of contract on a daily basis. Whether your contractual day starts with your bus or train ride to work in the morning, or the parking garage where you leave your car, and ends with the groceries you bring home in the evening, you enter into and perform a multitude of contracts throughout. You need not sign your name to a formal document to enter into a contract, as long as you have an offer from one party, an acceptance from another party, and some form of "consideration" that passes or will pass between the parties.

In order to form a contract, the parties must be legally able to enter into a binding agreement. Laws have been written to help govern us and for our protection from before the day we are born until after we die. Many a hotelier, tour operator, and retail agent has learned the hard way that a child below the age of maturity cannot be held to a contract and cannot be made to pay for anything except the necessities of life—food, clothing, and medical treatment. The supplier who has been convinced to send a teenager on a two-week vacation, and has learned too late of the inability of the minor to pay, has a hard time explaining to a court that he should be able to collect for what the minor has enjoyed. A child can only be legally made to pay for the basic necessities of life, and that, although I find disagreement within the travel industry, does not include two-week vacations at a resort.

If at some time you are giving refunds for services not performed for a minor, you should make sure to pay the legal guardian of the child, usually the parent, who was originally responsible for the debt. Paying the child does not discharge the debt, and you might have to pay all over again.

To add to the confusion, a person comes of age at different times for different purposes—and these various ages differ in different states. In most states, the age of majority is 18, while others use 19 or 21 as the age of majority. In many states, marriage terminates a person's minority, but this does not apply to serving alcoholic beverages. The hotel caught serving liquor to a minor may get its liquor license revoked.

A *void* contract has no legal effect between the parties and creates no legal rights or obligations (i.e., to sell illegal tours or products).

A *voidable* contract is capable of being disclaimed by one of the parties (i.e., the minor's trip).

An *unenforceable* contract may look good on its face but may not be allowed as against public policy or not signed by a party.

An *illegal* contract contravenes the law and is automatically void (i.e., to provide liquor or drugs to minors).

To illustrate the simplest form of contract for this chapter, let us assume the following transaction. Go to a restaurant and order a hamburger from the menu that costs $3.95 plus applicable sales taxes. The "consideration" passing between the parties is the food on the part of the restaurant and the payment of money on your part.

Assume that the menu does not show the price of each item and simply lists a variety of dishes, and you order without asking the price of the item. When your bill arrives for $15, with all of this good legal training instilled in you, you claim that the bill is outrageous, and you refuse to pay. When the owner comes over to explain that his normal charge for the item is $15, what basic contract law are you to rely on?

The applicable legal rule is that, when no price is mentioned, the reasonable value of the item is the amount that is due, and all this depends upon the circumstances involved. When the price is not initially mentioned, the law does not allow it to be arbitrarily set by either party at a later time. The only obligation to pay is that of the reasonable *value* involved.

Within all contracts, there are implied terms that must be followed. Let us assume that the food is so badly burnt, or so sour, that you would not even think of bringing it home to your pet. Within the implied terms is that, when you ordered the food, it is "fit to be eaten by human beings." If the food is so bad that it could not fit this implied category, you should not have any obligation to pay for it. The restaurant does not have the legal ability to say merely that you were the customer who ordered it and must pay when confronted with food that was not edible.

The unwritten words on the menu constitute what is known as an *implied warranty.* An implied warranty is as much a part of the contract as though it were printed on a menu. The warranty of fitness for a particular use is perhaps the most common of implied warranties.

In all contracts, there must be a meeting of the minds in a commonly accepted meaning of words. In the United States, when you order a hamburger you might appropriately believe that at least some part of the hamburger is beef from a cow, as compared to meat from a horse, which well might be acceptable in some foreign countries. The principle involved here is that the words of a contract, unless they deal with a highly technical subject, are always to be understood in their commonly accepted meanings.

Implied in the contract is timely delivery unless otherwise specified. Using the restaurant scenario again, you ordered the hamburger upon your arrival at 12:15, but an hour later the chef is still trying to figure out, "Where's the beef?"

When you explain to the waiter that you do not intend to pay for what you have not received, that you have to get back to work, and the manager comes up and states that nothing on the menu specified when your order would be delivered, you argue the theory of timely delivery. Since you went into the restaurant at a normal lunch period, it is reasonable to assume that your food should be served promptly.

From the above scenarios, you can see that even the simplest of transactions can become quite complicated. The simple item, "Hamburger ... $3.95" really means something like this: "We offer to deliver to you within a reasonable time, a hamburger consisting of some beef, that shall be clean and fit for human consumption, at the cost to you of $3.95."

Contracts must be sufficiently definite and certain to permit an appropriate remedy in the event of a breach. In the above example, we can see where such terms as price, time of performance, and size of the product may be implied by the courts.

How is an offer terminated? There are several ways:

1. Lapse of a stated time period;
2. Revocation by the offerer prior to acceptance by the offeree;
3. An impossibility of performance by law or by fact;
4. A rejection;
5. A counteroffer by the offeree;
6. Death of either party; or
7. Conditioned on an act that does not occur.

If an offer is made to you, and you answer that offer by a completely different offer, the original offer is terminated. If you merely suggest changes to the original offer or ask if the offerer would be interested in $2 less, this would not normally automatically reject an offer unless you use the words, "I will only give you $2 per item less than you are offering to me."

For the contract to exist, there must be a meeting of the minds. If there is a mistake by both parties as to the basic subject matter or the purpose of the contract, the courts will not enforce the contract.

If performance has become impossible, perhaps because of an item's destruction prior to the date it was to be turned over, performance will not be enforced by the courts.

If one of the parties has used fraud, or physical or economic duress, on the other, the party cannot use the courts to enforce this inequitable position. The normal remedy in such a situation is called *rescission* (voiding) of the complete contract, or, depending upon the wording, perhaps only the portions with offending provisions. The court will not enforce unconscionable clauses, that is, provisions that take unfair advantage of the other party or are so outrageous as to not allow the court to be a part of enforcement.

Must a contract be in writing to be enforceable? Many legal problems within the travel, tourism, and hospitality industries would be eliminated if the contracts actually were in writing. Under what is known as the *statute of frauds*, certain contracts (those for the sale of real property; those not to be performed within a year) must be in writing if they are to be enforced by the courts. In the travel industry, this is usually not a problem since most hotels' arrangements are for less than one year. In most states, leases for occupancy longer than one year must be in writing.

In most states, a contract for the sale of goods in an amount exceeding $500 must be in writing. Although it is questionable whether various travel services, such as transportation, would come within this $500 limit, when a retail agent or tour operator sells a package tour with various components, the argument may be made that the package constitutes "goods," and therefore arrangements must be in writing if the cost is more than $500. Although this amount fluctuates from as low as $30 to a couple of hundred dollars in certain states, must jurisdictions have placed a $500 limitation.

We are talking here about the enforceability of the statute of frauds in the courts, not whether the contract is legal or illegal. Generally, contracts that ought to be performed within one year must be in writing unless both parties can freely terminate them. Thus, a three-year contract to a hotel or travel agent must be in writing.

What should a written contract contain? The following six points should be understood and remembered. They will assist you with any business contracts you will be entering into.

The answers to the questions *who, what, why, where, how,* and *when* provide a complete and precise statement of the understanding of the parties:

1. ***Who***: Who the actual parties to the contract are. If it is a corporation, rather than an individual, requesting the services or transportation, state the exact capacity of the person forming the contract.
2. ***What***: What the precise terms or services being requested are. What the agreement seeks to accomplish. What each of the parties is to do, furnish, pay, or receive. What the parties assume, if anything, as to the basis of their agreement.
3. ***Why***: Why the parties are making the agreement.
4. ***Where***: Where the transportation is to be performed or notices to be given, where payment is to be made, where the contract is to be performed, where jurisdiction and venue is to take place, and thus where the contract is being made.
5. ***How***: How the parties will discharge their obligations to each other and how they will deal with events such as strikes, weather, acts of violence, inability of other suppliers to perform, death or sickness of one of the

parties, bankruptcy, or delays that are the fault of neither party.

6. ***When***: When transportation or services are to be performed and whether time is of the essence (if applicable). If the services are seasonal, with various rates that would change the prices, all this should be contained in the contract. If the services are for promotional transportation, excluded or "blacked out" periods during which the contract will not be applicable.

If a term in the contract is an *express term* that goes to the root of the contract, a *material breach* of this allows the innocent party to terminate the contract and receive damages.

For years, the relationship between the consumer and the travel agency has been one of basic oral contracts; very little is in writing other than an invoice or an itinerary summarizing the agreement of the parties. As a reminder for Preventive Legal Care®, the more terms and conditions set forth in writing on the invoices, ticket jackets, or some part of the agreement between the parties, the more likely it is that disputes can be avoided. More extensive use of consumer disclosure notices where legal or disclaimers appears to be a necessity, as litigation over unclear contractual terms continues to become increasingly prevalent. (The new Travel Directives for the European Union unfortunately prohibits the use of disclaimer notices.)

RESEARCH AND REVIEW

1. What are the requirements for a binding contract?
2. Describe consideration and how extensive it must be to bind an agreement.
3. Are only written contracts binding? Please explain your answer.
4. Describe the remedies available to both parties to a contract if there is a breach.

NOTES

CHAPTER 6

THE TRAVEL AGENT AND PROCEDURAL DUE PROCESS

The Fourth Amendment to the Constitution of the United States provides for protection against unreasonable searches and seizures. These protections have been held to be applicable to businesses and business records. Almost every state in the union has an identical provision in its respective state constitution. In addition to the individual protections under the various state constitutions, the protections of the Fourth Amendment are applied to the states through the provisions of the Fourteenth Amendment to the United States Constitution.

When considering the protections of the Fourth Amendment, you must also consider the guarantees of the Due Process Clause found in the Fifth Amendment. The Due Process Clause guarantees that a person shall

not be deprived of life, liberty, or property without due process of law. Numerous judicial decisions under the Due Process Clause have determined that due process means, most significantly "notice and the opportunity to be heard." Moreover, it is well established through judicial decisions that the word "persons" includes both individuals and corporations.

Travel agents should be aware of their constitutional rights and protections against unreasonable searches, inspections, and seizures from administrative agencies or carrier representatives. In addition to the constitutional guarantees, the agent is also protected by certain provisions and resolutions adopted by the ARC. Under the Agent Reporting Agreement, the agency's books and records shall be open for such inspection, and the authorized representative may make appropriate notes and copies. However, ARC/IATAN legally and ethically owe the travel agent an obligation of *procedural due process* in conducting their inspection. Procedural due process means that ARC or IATAN will conduct their inspections by (1) affording the travel agency reasonable notice and (2) allowing the travel agent the opportunity to respond in a reasonable manner, not only to the inspection request, but to any questions or accusations the inspector may make.

Whenever an agent is faced with a question of whether a search, inspection, or proposed seizure is constitutional or lawful, the first question is what constitutes reasonable notice. A practical definition of reasonable notice could be such notice that would permit the average person under similar circumstances the opportunity to diligently seek to protect his or her property rights. This would include the time necessary to consult with travel law counsel and to determine the exact nature of the rights and liabilities in question. Obviously, the more complex and extensive the records and data to be reviewed, the more advance notice should be given.

The agent should remember that the Office of Enforcement is only entitled to inspect those documents and materials relevant to the specific purpose of the examination. The agent should not be intimidated by the enforcement officer and should take the time necessary to separate the relevant material from that which is totally unrelated to the specific purpose of the examination.

If an agency is in jeopardy of being removed from the ARC's approved agency list, its plates and ticket stock seized, and, in effect, faced with the serious possibility of being shut down as a business, the economic survival of the agency is at stake, and a more extensive hearing is required.

The main lesson to be learned in a review of procedural due process requirements is to remain calm and to insist on the rights of an agency whenever the threat of an audit or inspection is presented. You should insist upon your right to reasonable notice, and also demand the opportunity to consult with an attorney to determine your rights.

RESEARCH AND REVIEW

1. Where are the travel agent's protections against unreasonable search and seizure to be found?
2. What should a travel agent do if ARC demands immediate access to all his/her records?

CHAPTER 7

JURISDICTION

As long as the world around us continues to change, the travel, tourism, and hospitality industries must adapt to these changes.

Because the law is an inexact branch of knowledge, our courts will continue to be overburdened with litigation and will continue to see decisions from eminent judges who disagree with each other. Within the law, there will always be guiding principles and precedents from the past that will assist us in interpreting the answers to legal problems.

Each of the 50 sovereign states of the United States has its own legislature and its own system of courts. State laws are subservient to federal laws, and we have at the top of the system the federal Congress and the federal courts. The Constitution of the United States is the source from which the powers of both federal and state legislatures are derived and by which their scope is limited. Our laws are made by either the enactment in legislatures, which would be *statutory law*, or by decisions in the courts, which is called *common law* or "case law."

The basic law of most of the United States is the common law of England, which was adopted in the early constitutions of the states as they were formed. (The only exception is the State of Louisiana, where the "code" system prevails as a result of the prior French influence. Statutory law, rather than case law, is thus the basic law of Louisiana.)

The laws enacted by the legislatures of the various states, and those passed by Congress, constitute our statutes, or "written law." The function of statutes is to modify the common law to suit changing times, to replace it if necessary, and to provide for situations not covered by the common law.

The courts are given the task of interpreting statutes drawn up by Congress or the legislatures. Cases and decisions involving statutes have the same value as cases and decisions based on common law. The travel industry deals with tourists, businesspeople, and industry personnel traveling throughout the world and is therefore involved in contracts and legal situations that may involve many jurisdictions.

Even though there is no international legislature with power to enforce its acts, there is very little in the way of international courts other than the informal international arbitral tribunals or the International Court of Justice at The Hague that, unfortunately, does not have the power to enforce its international decisions. International law affects almost every travel industry business to some extent. For example, if a United States traveler slips and falls while visiting a hotel in Bermuda, the court will apply principles of international law to determine whether the defendant can be sued in the United States, or whether suit must be brought in the foreign country in which the hotel is situated.

In one such case, the court ruled that the injured plaintiff had to bring suit in Bermuda, where the hotel was located, because the hotel hadn't conducted sufficient business, or otherwise "availed itself," of the benefits of the forum state—California—to have to defend itself there.[1]

The California court ruled that merely advertising the recreational activities/facilities in California did not generate sufficient California contacts to subject the hotel to personal jurisdiction in California for grievances occurring wholly outside of California.

Further, one of the most significant treaties relating to the travel industry, the Warsaw Convention, prescribes specifically where lawsuits may be brought for personal injury and property damage relating to commercial aviation. That treaty also provides for specific limits for lost or damaged baggage on international flights. (See Chapter 9.)

The basic laws within one jurisdiction may prove to be in conflict with the laws of other areas. The question as to which jurisdiction, or which venue, properly applies to your factual situation depends upon a number of factors. International laws have been formulated by international treaties, by decisions in the countries' respective courts, and by principles set down by scholars and experts on the subject. Through the efforts of the League of Nations following World War I and the United Nations after World War II, significant progress toward the establishment of a world court was formed where litigation between sovereign nations could be heard. Only through agreement of both parties can international arbitration be effective for members of the travel industry.

---

1. *See, e.g., Sklar v. Princess Properties International,* 194 Cal.App.3d 1202 (1987).

In the United States, the Constitution specifically gives Congress the right to make laws regarding interstate and foreign commerce and to deal with all matters having to do with interstate or foreign relations.

Under our Constitution, legislative power, not expressly delegated to the federal government and not prohibited by the Constitution, is reserved to the states. Unless a federal question is involved, or a question in which citizens of different states are involved, litigation must be brought to the state courts.

Laws passed by cities, towns, or counties derive their authority from the state constitution or the state legislature. Whether you can bring a suit against a defendant or be the plaintiff yourself in litigation against another party, must depend upon whether or not you have "jurisdiction" over the other person.

For example, you might not be able to bring a cause of action against a government that has sovereign immunity, which is the individual government's freedom from being sued for liability for acts arising from its governmental function. In the United States, if an airline is over 51 percent owned by a foreign government, you may sue the carrier in our federal courts, but you cannot have a trial by jury as you can in all other lawsuits.

In the United States, it is more difficult to sue the federal, state, or local government than to sue a private individual, but it can be done. Suing a foreign government within the United States is even more difficult, but, in certain circumstances, a government might lose its sovereign immunity.

Whenever the government or an individual officer acts outside the bounds of its lawful authority, jurisdiction may be appropriate. Normally, you would not be able to sue the government for errors government employees make *within* the bounds of their authority.

Suits against citizens and/or entities (corporations, associations, etc.) of foreign countries may be filed in either the federal courts or the courts of the particular state connected with the action.

The Due Process Clause of the Fourteenth Amendment limits the power of a state court to exert personal jurisdiction over a nonresident defendant. In order for a state court to have jurisdiction in a lawsuit over a foreign defendant, it must be shown that the defendant purposefully established "minimum contacts" in that state. Some examples of that conduct are marketing a product or service in that state, designing it for marketing in that state, establishing regular channels for providing regular advice to customers in that state, or advertising in that state.[2]

Many state laws provide that the courts of the particular state may exercise jurisdiction over a defendant, provided that it is not inconsistent with the Constitution of the United States or the constitution of that state.[3]

---

2. *Asahi Metal Industry Co. v. Cheng Shin Rubber Co.*, U.S. Supreme Court No. 85-698, Feb. 24, 1987.
3. *See, e.g.*, California Code of Civil Procedure, Section 410.10.

There are two components to jurisdiction: subject matter jurisdiction and personal jurisdiction. *Subject matter jurisdiction* means that the particular court has the authority to entertain the dispute in question.

Provided that the court has subject matter jurisdiction, it must obtain personal jurisdiction over the defendant. An important procedural requirement of *personal jurisdiction* is accomplished by serving the lawsuit and "summons" on the defendant. The summons notifies the defendant of the suit, and advises the period and manner in which the defendant must respond. Service of the lawsuit and summons may be done in California, for example, by either handing a copy of it to the defendant anywhere in the world, or, alternatively, by mailing a copy of the suit and summons by certified mail, return receipt requested. "Service" of the suit is then complete 10 days after such mailing.[4]

In any case, the strictures of the Due Process Clause of the United States Constitution forbid a state court from exercising personal jurisdiction over a nonresident person or entity if it would "offend traditional notions of fair play and substantial justice."[5] The determination of the reasonable exercise of jurisdiction in each case depends on several factors. A court must consider the burden on the defendant, the interests of the forum state, and the plaintiff's interest in obtaining relief. Courts must take into account the burdens placed upon defendants who must defend themselves in a foreign legal system. The Supreme Court has ruled in this regard:

> *In every case, however, those interests, as well as the federal interest in its foreign relations policies, will be best served by a*

---

4. Code of Civil Procedure, Section 415.40.
5. *Asahi Metal Industry Co. v. Cheng Shin Rubber Co., supra.*

> *careful inquiry into the reasonableness of the assertion of jurisdiction in the particular case, and an unwillingness to find the serious burdens on an alien defendant outweighed by minimal interests on the part of the plaintiff or the forum state. Great care and reserve should be exercised when extending our notions of personal jurisdiction into the international field.*[6]

Thus, as a Preventive Legal Care® measure, where a United States travel agency or other business enters into any agreement with a foreign-based business, it is wise to add language to the contract (even if just a letter agreement) specifying that any dispute arising in connection with the agreement or its performance "shall be resolved by the courts of [your own city and state]." If the only written "contract" is the check itself, write on the back of the check "acceptance of this check accepts [your own city or state] as the venue and jurisdiction for any disputes arising out of this contract."

RESEARCH AND REVIEW

1. Describe the requirements enabling you to sue a defendant in your jurisdiction.
2. How do you obtain jurisdiction over foreign travel business operators within your jurisdiction if they have no office, representative, or direct advertising in your area?
3. Name the various courts in your area and the jurisdictional limitations to bring suits in each.
4. Describe five Preventive Legal Care® theories to lessen potential legal problems.

---

6. Ibid.

NOTES

CHAPTER 8

ANTITRUST LAWS AND THE TRAVEL AGENT

A trust is defined as a combination of industrial or commercial companies or a large corporation exercising semimonopolistic control over some service or product. A monopoly exists when there is exclusive control of a commodity or service in a particular market, especially when that control makes it possible for the entity to manipulate prices. Monopolies and trusts are not favored by the law because they tend to eliminate competition.

In the United States, there are both federal and state laws that guard against the evils of monopolies and trusts. The basic federal statute is the Sherman Act. The Sherman Act was passed in 1890 and has been amended several times since that date. The Sherman

Act was complemented by the passage of the Clayton Act in 1914.

Section 1 of the Sherman Act states, in part: "Every contract, combination, or conspiracy of restraint in trade is hereby declared to be illegal." Section 2 of the Act prohibits the monopolization of an industry or attempts to monopolize.

Section 4 of the Clayton Act allows a person to recover triple the amount of damages for a proven civil antitrust violation. Similarly, the Sherman Act provides that a criminal violator may be subject to a fine of $1,000,000 and a jail term of three years.

In order to win on an attempt to monopolize claim, the plaintiff must show:

1. A "specific intent" to monopolize a particular, and relevant, market;
2. Predatory acts designed to achieve that objective; and
3. A "dangerous probability" of success in achieving a monopoly in the relevant market.

It should be noted that the antitrust statutes only prohibit unreasonable restraints of trade. While there are numerous types of trade restraints, the courts have identified four specific categories in which restraints of trade are *per se* (automatically) unreasonable. This means that the actions will be prohibited and are illegal regardless of the specific motive or even effect of a particular action. The categories of *per se* violations are:

1. Agreements between competitors to control prices;
2. Agreements between competitors to divide markets for customers;
3. Agreements between competitors to boycott other businesses; and

4. "Tie-ins." A tie-in exists when the seller of a highly desired good or service requires the purchaser to buy another distinct good or service. In order for an illegal tie-in to occur the two products must be substantially different. If one product is merely a component of the second, then no tie-in has occurred.

Agreements between competitors to set or control the price of goods or services is commonly known as *price fixing*. It is no defense to a Sherman Act charge that the price established was a reasonable price or that such price was agreed upon to prevent ruinous or cut-throat competition.[1] In reaching this policy, this court has determined that any type of price fixing in the short run may allow the price fixers to gain control of the market in the long run.

---

1. *United States v. Trenton Potteries* (1927) 273 U.S. 392 and *Kiefer-Stewart v. Seagram* (1951) 340 U.S. 211.

The act only prohibits competitors from reaching agreements to control, fix, or tamper with prices. Where the competitors individually match each other's prices, and do not agree to do so, no Sherman Act violation has occurred. This mere matching of prices by competitors, without any agreement to do so, is known as "conscious parallelism," and does not violate the antitrust laws.[2] This is not illegal because, among other reasons, it is natural for competitors to individually set their prices to be competitive with the lowest price offered for a given product or service.

For example, if one carrier establishes a low-priced fare on a major route, say, Los Angeles to New York, other competing carriers will usually immediately match that fare. This is "conscious parallelism" in pricing by competitors, and does not violate the law. However, if representatives of major air carriers sat down at a table, or phoned each other and agreed that they would each establish their fares at *any* level (not necessarily at the same level), that would violate the Sherman Act. Again, the reason is because price "tampering" by competitors is *per se* illegal.

The antitrust statutes also prohibit competitors from reaching agreements to fix the terms and conditions of the sales of goods and services or to limit the production of such goods or services. Since supply and demand are closely related, a control over the supply of certain goods or services would allow the producers to artificially control the price of those goods and services. For example, it has been held illegal for an association of travel agents to agree on standard cancellation charges.[3]

---

2. *Theatre Enterprises, Inc. v. Paramount Film Distributing Corp.*, 346 U.S. 537 (1954).
3. *United States v. Orange County Travel Agents Association*, Civil No.75-1513 WAB (C.D. Cal. 1975) Consent Decree Entered.

A *group boycott* exists where businesspeople band together and agree not to deal with another business where there is evidence of some sort of anticompetitive motive.[4] For example, if travel agencies grouped together and refused to sell a certain wholesaler's tour because the wholesaler refused to pay group members an override commission they had demanded, it would be considered a group boycott.

It is also illegal for competitors to divide markets (geographically and otherwise) among themselves. This is known as *horizontal* market allocation. Horizontal means that the agreement or allocation is made between competitors on the same level of distribution. Horizontal agreements are those, for example, between manufacturers, or between wholesalers/distributors, or between retailers themselves. A *vertical* agreement, by contrast, is one between members of different levels of distribution, such as an agreement between a wholesaler and retailer concerning the price at which the retailer will resell the product. When competitors agree that they will not sell goods or services outside their own territory, this constitutes a horizontal territorial allocation and is a *per se* violation of the Sherman Act. Travel agents who agree among themselves not to solicit customers within certain territories or classes of customers could easily be charged with antitrust violations.

Under the federal and state antitrust laws, only unreasonable restraints of trade are illegal, known as the "Rule of Reason." Of course, as already explained, some categories of restraints have been deemed by the United States Supreme Court to be *per se* illegal—that is, they are always considered to be illegal, regardless of the reason for the restraint. If a restraint is deemed to be reasonable, to serve a particular business or social purpose, then the restraint is not illegal. The court will

---

4. *Klor's, Inc. v. Broadway Hale Stores* (1959) 359 U.S. 207.

consider various factors in determining the reasonableness of any particular restraint of trade:

1. The restraint and its relationship to the specific business concerned;
2. The history of the development of the restraint;
3. The reasons behind the adoption of the restraint; and
4. The balance between the need or desire for the restraint against the hardships or benefits to society.

In reaching its determination regarding the Rule of Reason, the court will look to any less restrictive alternatives that may be available to the manufacturer. The court will also look closely to see that the restraint proposed is reasonably related to the purported goal.

When the U.S. Civil Aeronautics Board (CAB) was in existence, the associations of domestic and international airlines [the Air Traffic Conference (ATC) and the International Air Transport Association (IATA)] were afforded immunity from the antitrust laws, provided they first obtained approval of their "resolutions" (rules) dealing with travel agents from the Civil Aeronautics Board.

When the CAB was disbanded on December 31, 1984, ATC was also disbanded (as well as the travel agent arm of IATA) and replaced with the Airlines Reporting Corporation (ARC) and the International Airlines Travel Agent Network (IATAN). There is no provision for filing these entities' rules or regulations with the U.S. Department of Transportation, or other United States government agency, in order to obtain antitrust immunity. These organizations operate without antitrust immunity.

Principally because the ARC Agreement contains some "due process" protections for travel agents who violate ARC rules, the Antitrust Division of the U.S. Justice Department issued a "Business Review Letter" stating that it would not take government antitrust enforcement action against the operations of ARC. Because ARC and IATAN are composed of collections of individual competitor airlines, they are ready-made "combinations." Any actions by those combinations that "unreasonably restrain trade" would violate Section One of the Sherman Act. Although the United States government has indicated that it will not challenge the operations of ARC on antitrust grounds, private individuals or businesses that are injured by acts of ARC (or IATAN) may bring civil antitrust lawsuits against those entities for violations of antitrust laws.

RESEARCH AND REVIEW

1. Explain the purpose of antitrust legislation.
2. What are the pertinent federal antitrust statutes that apply to the travel industry?
3. What types of antitrust suits have we seen in the travel industry?
4. Describe a *per se* antitrust violation, and list as many examples as you can.
5. As an agency owner or tour operator, what steps would you take to prevent an antitrust suit from being brought against you?
6. What are the penalties for antitrust violations?
7. Explain the "Rule of Reason."

NOTES

CHAPTER 9

BAGGAGE LIABILITY FOR AIR CARRIERS

The liability of an air carrier for lost or damaged baggage is governed by two different sets of rules. One set of rules applies to baggage that is lost or damaged during international travel; the other applies to baggage lost or damaged during domestic travel.

International baggage liability is governed by the provisions of the Warsaw Treaty. In 1929, the Warsaw Convention was held in Poland to unify the rules relating to international air transportation. In 1963, a protocol following a convention at The Hague, Netherlands, became effective. The primary effect of the protocol was to increase the limits of liability for carriers. Although The Hague protocol has no effect in the United States, it is important that travel personnel understand the rules and regulations of the protocol so that they can advise the many international travelers who have contact with the United States.

Under the terms of the Warsaw Convention, a carrier is only responsible for checked baggage or goods. If baggage or goods are checked with the carrier and a loss or damage occurs during transportation by air, the air carriers will be liable for the loss. The period of transportation by air is not limited to the actual flight, but extends to the period during which baggage or goods are in the charge of the carrier, whether in an airport or on board the aircraft. However, if the baggage is lost or is damaged during a cab ride to the airport or on an independent bus shuttle or ferry ride to other points outside the airport, the carrier will not normally be liable under the Warsaw Convention. Liability for loss occurring to baggage or goods that occurs during transportation by land, sea, or river is governed by other statutes or common law.

One of the major advantages to the air carrier is the limits on liability imposed by the Warsaw Convention. In the case of checked baggage or goods, liability is limited to a sum of about U.S. $9.07 per pound, unless the passenger has made a declaration of excess value at the time the package was delivered to the carrier and paid any necessary premiums for additional insurance coverage. In such cases, the carrier will be liable for any sum up to the declared sum.

With regard to carry-on baggage, the liability of a carrier is limited to 5000 francs (about $52) per passenger regardless of the number of carry-on articles.

If the carrier proves that the damage was caused by or contributed to by the negligence of the passenger, a court may exonerate the carrier of liability entirely, or partly.[1] Still, passengers should always check to insure that they follow all instructions regarding proper labeling and identification of their baggage and the security of all locks and fasteners.

---

1. Warsaw Convention, Article 21.

The Warsaw Convention also provides a very unique consumer protection provision. Article 23 of the Convention expressly provides that a carrier contract that attempts to relieve the carrier of liability, or limit its liability by contract less than the limits expressly stated by the Convention, shall be void. Any provision intending to relieve the carrier of liability or to fix a lower limit than that which is allowed shall be deemed null and void.

Also under the terms of the Warsaw Convention, an air carrier must meet certain requirements relating to liability limitations. First, the air carrier must deliver a baggage check for all transported baggage, other than small personal items carried aboard and controlled by the passenger. The baggage check must be numbered, contain the number and weight of the packages, and a statement that the transportation is subject to the rules relating to liability established by the Convention. Second, a carrier will not be allowed to avail itself of the provisions of baggage liability if the damage is caused by willful misconduct of the carrier.

Liability for loss or damage to baggage during domestic transportation is governed by the terms of the economic regulations of the Department of Transportation.[2] The economic regulations establish limits on liability for any flight using large aircraft; that is, aircraft that contain more than 60 passenger seats. The regulations also govern any flight segment that is included on the same ticket as another flight segment that uses large aircraft. Similar to the provisions of the Warsaw Convention, a carrier cannot limit its liability from the loss, delay, or damage to baggage in an amount less than $1,250 per passenger, if direct or consequential damages can be proved.

As of November 1, 1994, the Department of Transportation proposed to raise the minimum limit on compensation for lost or damaged baggage from $1,250 per passenger on domestic flights to $1,850.

The DOT also sought comment on alternative proposals. One would raise the minimum limit to $1,850 per passenger, with future increases "tied to the rise in consumer prices," the DOT said. The second would raise the minimum to $2,000. Passengers still would be required to prove claims for damages under the proposals.

The minimum is intended to strike a balance between covering passenger losses and protecting airlines from excessive claims. Today's $1,250 limit was set 10 years ago.

When the passenger uses the services of two or more different airlines during the trip, the airline that carried the passenger to his ultimate destination is responsible for lost or damaged baggage. Applying this rule, the passenger has superior protection because the rule remains in effect even if the passenger has changed carriers and the first line caused the loss, or if the passenger changes his mind in mid-journey and connects

---

2. *See* Volume 14, Section 254, of the Code of Federal Regulations.

to a different line from that originally scheduled. Also similar to the Warsaw Convention, the economic regulations require that notice of any monetary limitation on baggage liability be printed conspicuously with the ticket or on the ticket itself.

In cases where baggage has been lost or misplaced, the agent should advise the customer to immediately file a claim with the carrier and, if insured, to make sure an insurance claim is also filed. The agent should also establish that the customer has presented a valid passenger's claim check and a full description of the missing articles. The agent should then examine the claim check to make sure it has the proper destination listed and also check to match the flight information with the information on the claim check. If an incorrect destination is listed, the agent can contact the receiving station and request that the baggage be forwarded.

Since almost all airlines now maintain some type of computerized baggage-tracing facilities and communications network, it is much easier to trace lost or misplaced baggage. The computer network enables the agent at one destination to send forwarding messages to a second destination once an article has been located and properly identified.

In cases where the missing article cannot be immediately located, the airline will usually assume the expense of delivery of the delayed baggage. Tariff regulations mandate that the carrier compensate the passenger for all reasonable and documented expenses incurred as a result of loss or delay in the delivery of this baggage. If same-day delivery is impossible, most carriers will provide an overnight kit containing essential toiletries for the passenger. If the baggage is still missing the next day, most station agents are authorized by the carrier to compensate the passenger for small necessities such as new underwear, a change of shirt, or laundry costs. However, most carriers provide supervisors to approve any large expenditures, and the passenger will be required to present receipts. Passengers must bear in mind that they are only entitled to reasonable expenses.

If the airline is unable to locate the baggage after a six-week period, the passenger must be compensated with either the value of the missing item or an amount equal to the maximum liability, whichever is less. Disgruntled passengers have also been able to recover damages for lost valuables under general contract principles. For example, the court determined that an airline is obligated to tell its passengers of its practice of delaying transport of passenger baggage so that it can accommodate additional passengers. In *Lowell Glen Daun v. Sun Aire Airlines*,[3] the court found that Sun Aire deliberately failed to transport the plaintiff's baggage with his flight in order to accommodate additional passengers. Since the plane had limited capacity, it was the carrier's usual procedure on weekend flights from San Francisco to Las Vegas to load additional passengers and fly the luggage later, on emptier planes. Since the airline failed to disclose this practice, the passenger was unable to make alternate arrangements and suffered damages when his baggage was delayed. The plaintiff was allowed to recover his actual and consequential damages.

It is highly advisable for travel agents to encourage their customers to purchase travel insurance, which normally provides coverage for lost baggage and personal possessions. If baggage is lost, travelers having insurance will then look to their insurer for compensation, and not to the travel agency.

RESEARCH AND REVIEW

1. Describe all the international restrictions on recovery for lost or stolen baggage.
2. Explain domestic recovery restrictions.

3. 17 Avi. L. Rpts (CCH) 17,536 (1982).

CHAPTER 10

AIRLINE OVERBOOKING

The law regarding compensation to passengers who are denied boarding by the carrier after having reserved a seat has expanded greatly in the last few years. Starting with the landmark Nader case,[1] the courts have fashioned various rules regarding compensation to passengers who are bumped from their flights.

Over the past few years, disgruntled customers have been allowed to recover damages based on theories of breach of contract, misrepresentation, a private right of action, request for punitive damages, and discrimination.

Prior to its demise at the end of 1984, the Civil Aeronautics Board rewrote its boarding priority rules that had been in effect since 1978. In Part 250 of the Economic Regulations, the Board set down various

1. *Nader v. Allegheny Airlines, Inc.* (1976) 426 U.S. 290.

guidelines for procedures to be followed by the air carrier when a flight has been overbooked. Perhaps, to be politically correct, we should call it "underdeparted," not overbooked.

The first step in addressing the problem in an overbooked flight is a request by the carrier for volunteers to surrender their seats. A volunteer is a person who responds to the carrier's request and who is willing to accept the carrier's offer of compensation in exchange for relinquishing the confirmed reserved space. All the other passengers denied boarding are considered to have done so on an involuntary basis, even if the passenger accepts the denied boarding compensation offered by the carrier.

If there are not enough volunteers, the carrier may deny boarding to other passengers in accordance with its boarding priority rules.

Under the regulations, every carrier must establish priority rules and criteria for determining which passengers holding confirmed space will be denied boarding on an oversold flight if there aren't enough volunteers available. The boarding priority rules should minimize involuntary denied boarding and should be written so that the average person can understand them. Moreover, the air carrier cannot give unreasonable preference to any particular group or person.

As compensation to passengers denied boarding on an involuntary basis, the carrier may offer free or reduced rate transportation instead of a cash payment. However, the value of the transportation benefit should be equal to or greater than a cash payment as required by the regulations.

If passengers insist upon a cash payment, they are entitled to compensation at the rate of 200 percent of the sum of the value of travel to the passenger's next stopover or, if none, to the passenger's final destination, up to a maximum of $400. Another alternative is compensation in the amount of one-half the amount described above, with a $200 maximum, if the carrier arranges comparable air transportation which is intended to arrive at the passenger's next stopover or destination not later than two hours after the originally scheduled arrival time.

In any event, every carrier shall provide any passenger who is denied boarding on an involuntary basis a written statement explaining the terms, conditions, and limitations of denied boarding compensation. This written explanation must also be given to any person who requests such information at the airport from a ticket agent or representative of the carrier.

As the competition among the various airlines increased as a result of deregulation, consumers became more aware of the industry's deliberate overbooking practices. The rights of consumers were given a big boost by Ralph Nader's victory against Allegheny Airlines after he was involuntarily bumped from a scheduled flight and missed a speaking engagement. Nader's claim against the airline included a cause of action for common law fraudulent misrepresentation arising from Allegheny's failure to advise him of its deliberate overbooking practices. Fraudulent misrepresentation is the making of an untrue statement with knowledge of its falsity, and the intent to deceive another, that is justifiably relied upon by the other, to his or her detriment. In this case, the "statement" was confirming the reservation, while the carrier knew that, due to its policy of overbooking flights, the passenger holding the reservation might not be boarded. Nader was eventually awarded compensatory damages along with $25,000 in punitive damages against the airline, and the court's award was upheld in various appeals, that went all the way to the United States Supreme Court.

In 1983, in the case of *Goranson v. TWA*,[2] the court held the airline liable under a breach of contract theory when a passenger was bumped from a scheduled flight that was part of a vacation tour for which the passenger had contracted. The court held that the Federal Aviation Act did not protect airlines from a state law breach of contract clause, and the denied boarding compensation rules, established by the CAB, were not intended to be the exclusive remedy for damages resulting from a passenger being denied boarding on an involuntary basis.

Thus, under current law, when a flight is overbooked, the carrier must first request volunteers for denied boarding, who will accept compensation in exchange for relinquishing their confirmed reserved space. The compensation offered must be twice the value of their remaining flight coupons to the passenger's next stopover, or, if none, to his/her final destination, up to a maximum of $400. However, if the carrier arranges for air transportation that will arrive at the

2. 18 Avi L. Rpts. 17,637 (White Plains City Court, New York, 1983).

passenger's destination not later than two hours after a domestic flight originally booked, or four hours after an international flight, then the maximum cash payment that must be offered is $200.

Carriers may offer free or reduced rate air transportation in lieu of cash if the value of the transportation is equal to or greater than the cash payment otherwise required and the carrier informs the passenger of the amount of cash compensation that would otherwise be due. The passenger may decline the transportation benefit and receive the cash payment.

Passengers declined boarding are not required to accept the carrier's offer of compensation as their sole remedy. They may decline payment and seek damages in a court of law.

It is a sound Preventive Legal Care® measure for travel agents and tour operators to post notices and otherwise include warnings with passenger travel documents advising that flights may be overbooked. The Airlines Reporting Corporation provides all travel agents with a warning regarding the possibility of overbooking which it requests agents to display conspicuously.

RESEARCH AND REVIEW

1. Are air carriers allowed to overbook a potential flight?
2. What procedures must an air carrier follow when more passengers with confirmed reservations present themselves for a flight than there are seats available?
3. Explain the eligibility requirements to be entitled to denied boarding compensation.
4. Must a passenger accept the compensation offered by the carrier for involuntary denied boarding?

NOTES

CHAPTER 11

CLASS ACTION LITIGATION

A class action is a procedure by which one or more persons may bring a lawsuit and seek damages or other relief on behalf of themselves *and* all other persons who have been similarly damaged. In such cases, the actual people named in the lawsuit are referred to as the "named plaintiffs" or "named defendants." All other persons in similar situations are referred to as the "plaintiff class" or the "defendant class." A class action may be brought in federal court if it meets the requirements specified in Rule 23 of the Federal Rules of Civil Procedure. Many states also have very similar rules regarding class actions within their respective courts.

Before a person is allowed to institute a class action, it must be demonstrated to the court that the case meets the requirements for a class action. If this is successfully demonstrated, the case will be "certified" by the court as a class action, and the named plaintiff will be allowed to proceed. If the court refuses to certify the class, the named plaintiff will only be allowed to proceed on his or her own individual case.

It is important to note that most class actions are brought seeking a relatively small recovery for each individual. Since the potential recovery on an individual basis would not justify the time and expense of litigation, a failure to certify a class often means that the lawsuit will be dismissed or that the plaintiff will not follow through with litigating the matter.

The four major requirements that must be demonstrated in a class action are: (1) numerosity; (2) typicality; (3) common interest; and (4) adequacy of representation.

In the usual situation, the named plaintiff will meet the *numerosity* requirement by demonstrating that the class would be so large and have so many members that their participation in the proceedings would be impossible or extremely burdensome on the court. However, class actions have been certified for classes as few as 13 members up to classes of several thousand or even several million class members. Likewise, the damages suffered by each class member may range from a few dollars to several thousand dollars.

The second requirement of *typicality* requires that the named parties have claims or defenses that are typical of those of the various members of the class.

The third requirement is that of a *common interest* among the individual members of the class. The common interest will be demonstrated by showing a common question of law or facts for each member that would be addressed during the litigation. The common questions of law or fact must predominate over the individual questions of law or fact for the respective class members.

The fourth requirement, *adequacy of representation*, requires that the named parties be able to represent the interests of the class as a whole. A class action will require numerous hours of preparation and litigation, and the named parties must have sufficient counsel and resources to adequately protect the interests of the class of which they are members.

CONSUMER CLASS ACTIONS

The recent development of consumer advocate groups, coupled with federal and state legislation giving victims of fraudulent or unfair business practices specific legal rights to compensation, have resulted in an increase in filings in class action lawsuits by consumers. In 1971, the California Supreme Court permitted a class action to proceed on behalf of all persons who had been overcharged for taxicab service by the defendant company during a four-year period.[1] In its ruling, the court specifically addressed the possibility that, unless a class action suit was allowed, recovery by any individual member of the class was unlikely. The court was willing to extend the class action protection to those individuals rather than risk allowing a defendant to benefit from its alleged wrongdoing.

In the *Neilan v. Value Vacations, Inc.* class action, consumers who had purchased travel services from Value Vacations, Inc., consisting primarily of transportation on Arrow Air, filed suit against the defunct tour operator and several banks that had escrow agreements with the tour operator.[2] Those banks released the passengers' funds prematurely to the air carrier. The tour packages consisted of approximately 102 flights between the United States and Europe during the period May 1984 through January 1985. The tour operator, air carrier, and two banks entered into an escrow

1. *Daar v. Yellow Cab Company,* 67 Cal.2d 695, 433 P.2d 732, 63 Cal.Rptr. 724 (1967).
2. *Neilan v. Value Vacations, Inc.* (No. 84 Civ. 6672, 20 CCH Avi. L. Rpts. 17,176), U.S. District Court, S.D. N.Y. (Feb. 11, 1987).

agreement for deposit of consumer funds, and release of funds to the air carrier and tour operator as the flights were operated.

The court certified a class of almost 10,000 individuals, and refused to dismiss the claim against the defendant banks, holding that they had prematurely distributed escrow funds to the air carrier. The banks entered into a settlement with the plaintiff class, the evidence having shown that the banks violated federal regulations relating to disbursements for air charter operations.

In the *Guadagno* case, the court certified a class of approximately 400 persons who sought compensation from the owners of a Jamaican resort, their exclusive marketing agent, and various travel tour wholesalers and retailers who solicited the plaintiffs' purchase of charter tours to Jamaica.[3]

As the court stated:

> *The circumstances of this case, involving a cohesive and finite group of similarly situated vacationers, who relied upon essentially the identical representations in advertising matter, are amenable to class action treatment.*
>
> [*C*]*lass action relief may well be necessary to vindicate the rights of members of the class, whose individual claims are otherwise too small (under $500) to warrant independent litigation against the impressive legal strength of the defendants.*
>
> *Furthermore and perhaps most importantly, there are preponderant questions of law and fact sufficiently similar so that adjudication by* [*class*] *representation will be appropriate.*

---

3. *Guadagno v. Diamond Tours & Travel, Inc.*, 392 N.Y.S. 2d 783 (Supreme Court, N.Y. County, 1976).

In other class action lawsuits, the courts have specifically recognized the value of consumer class actions as probably the best method of avoiding a large number of lawsuits based upon the same wrongful act where the individual losses to the consumer are not substantial enough to warrant an expenditure of time and effort in proceeding with litigation. By combining small claims, the cost of litigation is prorated among numerous litigants, thereby making a lawsuit economically feasible. In the long run class action procedure gives injured consumers collective access to the courts and serves to deter improper conduct by sellers, who may face significant legal costs as well as large judgments or settlements in a consumer class action.

Travel agents and travel industry personnel, as part of an industry that affects millions of people, should be aware of the possibility of class action lawsuits filed by disgruntled travel consumers. Travel agents should carefully utilize all available consumer disclosure notices to specifically disclaim liability for the fault of others. When there is a question regarding the liability of the travel agent, a careful determination regarding the facts of each particular complaint should be made. It may be prudent to offer a small amount for settlement of a disputed claim rather than risk large expenditures participating in a class action lawsuit. The travel agent should also be aware of the protection offered by errors and omissions policies available through various insurance carriers.

RESEARCH AND REVIEW

1. Define the legal theory of class action litigation.
2. List the general court requirements for class action litigation.
3. List five examples of potential travel industry class action cases.
4. Describe the types of class action cases that have occurred within the travel industry.

CHAPTER 12

HOTEL AND HOSPITALITY LAW

Ever since early man decided to travel from where he was to where he wasn't, he has looked for a place where he could find temporary shelter and nourishment while on his voyage. From a small hut with a broom in front, stuck upside-down in the dirt, to today's huge hotel chains, the travel lodging industry still provides many of the basic services for the weary traveler. In the process, a large body of law has grown up, setting forth the rights, duties, and obligations of the various parties.

What is a hotel? Today, the words "hotel," "inn," and "motel" are synonymous for most legal purposes. Legal definitions vary from state to state, but most are quite similar, deriving as they do from the common law. A modern hotel is the descendant of the traditional inn—in other words, a building in which travelers, or transients, can expect to find temporary accommodation, as well as food, drink, and possibly entertainment.

One of the earliest English cases[1] required that the innkeeper must receive his guest, give him lodging and assistance, and keep his guest and his goods safe. It also gave the innkeeper a right of lien against his guest's goods for reasonable payment for such services. A *lien* is a legal interest in the property of another to secure payment of a debt owed to the "lienholder." The property may normally not be transferred to another until the debt is paid. Frequently, the property may be sold by the lienholder according to established procedures, if the debtor ultimately fails to pay the obligation. That, basically, remains the law today. It doesn't matter what words are in the title of the establishment—whether it calls itself a hotel, motel, inn, or whatever—the courts look to its function rather than its name to determine its legal status. Somewhat similar establishments, such as apartment-hotels, are not usually included in the definition of a hotel, due to the difference in the nature of the relationship between the landlord and the tenants as compared with a traveler and his place of rest.

INNKEEPER-GUEST RELATIONSHIPS: DUTIES OF AN INNKEEPER

When the tired traveler checks in for the night, a complex relationship between the guest and the proprietor of the inn is created, a relationship leading to rights and duties on both sides. The innkeepers assume the greater burden, as they are the ones providing the service. They undertake a number of legal obligations. The first and foremost obligation is to receive all guests who seek accommodation, up to the limits of the inn's capacity. This duty extends to all travelers, and especially to those who have an advance reservation. It is also applicable at any time of the day or night. Innkeepers also

1. *Cayle*, 77 Eng. Rep. 520.

have a duty to accept the guest's reasonable amount of luggage and find secure shelter for that as well.

Innkeepers may not turn away any traveler on the basis of race, creed, color, or place of national origin. Such discrimination is illegal, not only under the common law, but by statutory law in most state jurisdictions, and under federal jurisdiction. Additionally, a violation of this basic law can now result in criminal sanctions being sought against innkeepers, as well as civil litigation with punitive damages.

However, innkeepers do not have to take literally everybody who shows up at the door. There are some exceptions to the basic law of reception. One is if the prospective guest is not in a sober and orderly condition. Under common law, a person with an obvious communicable disease can be turned away (although the innkeeper may have a duty to assist such person in finding other shelter and appropriate medical assistance). Various state, federal and local laws now protect the traveler from discrimination on the basis of sexual preference, serious "social diseases" or physical or mental impairments. Innkeepers may determine that the prospective guest is able to pay for the accommodations and may require payment for all or a portion of the first night in advance. Another major exception is, of course, if the hotel is already full and has no more accommodations to let. A guest has the right only to available accommodation, which today usually means a private bedroom. He has no right to insist on sleeping on the pool table, on the couch in the lobby, or in a bathtub. Additionally, although innkeepers must allow the guest to bring in reasonable baggage, that is, items customarily brought into an inn, they don't have to permit unusual or extraordinary luggage, either in form or in quantity. Most jurisdictions now require that the inn keep a register, in which the names and usual addresses of their guests are recorded.

The problem of invited nonguests, or the guests of a guest, is a constantly thorny one. An innkeeper may exclude such persons if they are present for illegal or immoral purposes, or are engaging in obnoxious or undesirable conduct. However, the duties and obligations of an innkeeper may well extend towards someone who is visiting a guest.

Another important duty of innkeepers is that of providing suitable accommodations. They must furnish food and lodging that could reasonably be expected to be found at that particular inn, i.e., not slops and the broom closet. Additionally, innkeepers are held at law to have direct control over their rooms. Therefore they are also required to keep the rooms clean and the toilets sanitized, to provide a clean or sterile glass and fresh soap, clean linens, and so forth. Many states have now codified these requirements. The hotel that failed to clean a needle from the floor that injured a guest was held responsible.

Courteous treatment toward their guests is a traditional duty imposed on innkeepers and their employees and agents. Any substantial breach of this duty can lead to civil liability. Therefore, from a legal as well as a good business viewpoint, it is essential that the hotel's employees remain courteous and polite to the hotel's guests at all times.

One by-product of running an inn or hotel is handling the flow of the guests' messages and mail. Innkeepers have a duty toward their guests in this area as well. Usually it is handled in a routine manner, but some procedures should be worked out, such as writing down all telephone messages so that they can be given to the guest upon his return.

One of an innkeeper's most important duties toward guests is that of safety. Innkeepers must ensure the safety of a guest and his baggage. Some aspects of this have been codified in virtually all jurisdictions, and failure to comply may result in criminal as well as civil liability. For example, an innkeeper has a duty to see that fire escapes and fire extinguishers are at hand and in working order. Many jurisdictions now require hotels to install a thorough and effective sprinkler system. In fact, all aspects of fire prevention are among the most important and critical of an innkeeper's duties to maintain a safe environment. Failure to maintain an adequate fire defense may not only result in civil liability if there is an accident, but may also subject the innkeeper to criminal penalties, including a jail sentence. Hotels have been held liable for a headboard falling and injuring a guest since they had a duty to provide reasonably safe furnishings and premises. If a guest is robbed or attacked, it will be a question for the judge or jury as to whether the hotel was negligent.

Innkeepers also have a limited duty to protect their guests from harm caused by other guests or third parties. They must therefore maintain an adequate security system, depending on the nature of their establishment and its location. In this vein, the innkeeper also has supervisory responsibilities, to make sure that the guests behave in an appropriate and orderly fashion, to try to prevent one drunken or disorderly guest from injuring another guest. This is not to be interpreted as an automatic insurance policy or a strict liability standard, but merely a negligence standard for the "reasonable person" in a similar community and situation. This means that innkeepers will not be held liable without some *fault* on their part. They will only be held liable if they are negligent in their conduct towards the safety of the guests. A party is negligent, when he or she carelessly breaches a duty of due care that the law implies is owed by one to another under a given set of circumstances.

"Strict liability" means that the law imposes responsibility on one party for damage suffered by another, *regardless of fault*. In other words, the party upon whom the standard of strict liability is imposed becomes, in essence, an insurer. This standard is used most commonly in liability for the manufacture of defective products. It is not applicable to the provision of travel or hotel services.

Innkeepers also have the duty to keep their establishment as safe as possible, to avoid actions arising from their own negligence. This includes both the physical establishment and the actions of individuals, such as hotel employees. With regard to the physical establishment, innkeepers must maintain the premises in a safe condition and warn guests when something extraordinary occurs. Floors, balconies, stairs, and the like should be kept in a safe condition, clean and well lighted. Swimming pools are a particular source of concern, and care must be taken to be sure that they are well maintained and properly policed or posted with restrictions. Guests should be thoroughly warned when an unsafe condition exists, such as during repair or remodeling work. Normally this duty extends toward areas a guest would normally be in and not to areas outside of guest's normal use. In this day and age, however, innkeepers should try to keep their entire establishment in sufficiently good order to avoid liability for their negligence. They should not think that an affirmative defense, such as assumption of risk or contributory negligence, will save them.

An *affirmative defense* is one that a defendant in a lawsuit must raise and prove ("affirmatively") in order to escape or diminish that defendant's liability. *Assumption of risk* is such a defense, and lies where a defendant, with full knowledge of an extraordinary risk imposed by a certain activity, "assumes the risk of the activity," and proceeds anyway. That individual cannot later hold even a negligent party responsible, since that individual chose to engage in the risky activity, knowing the risk presented.

Contributory negligence and "comparative" negligence are affirmative defenses to lawsuits raised by a defendant where the plaintiff's own negligent act or acts caused or contributed to the event causing the plaintiff's injury. For example, this defense would be asserted by a hotel sued by a guest who slipped on a wet hotel walkway, injuring himself, while obviously intoxicated. The hotel might have been negligent in not properly maintaining the walkway, but the fact that the guest was clearly inebriated might bar ("contributory negligence") or partially diminish ("comparative negligence") the plaintiff's recovery.

Innkeepers are also responsible for their own conduct and that of their employees, as these bear on the safety of the guests. If a guest is injured by an employee acting in the course and scope of his/her employment, innkeepers are also responsible to the guest. However, if the employee is clearly acting outside such scope, the employee alone, and not the innkeeper, may be liable, unless the innkeeper was negligent in choosing or keeping such an employee. The test used by the courts to determine liability in such cases is the standard of reasonable care in negligence. Innkeepers must use "reasonable care" in keeping their premises safe and secure, or that amount of care used by a "reasonable person" in a like or similar condition, i.e., being an innkeeper. However, statutory liability of a stricter standard may be imposed on innkeepers in various jurisdictions.

The case of 18-year-old Thomas Hook illustrates a judicial perspective on the liability of innkeepers.[2] In this case, an inexperienced diver was injured when he dove from the three-meter diving board into shallow water at the Sheraton Park Hotel in Washington, D.C. The United States Court of Appeals for the District of Columbia stated the obligation of a hotel for the safety of its guests and the obligation of guests to exercise care for their own safety as follows:

---

2. *Hooks. v. Washington Sheraton,* 578 F. 2d 313 (D.C. Cir. 1977).

> *The owner of a hotel is not an insurer of the safety of his guests, but he does owe to them the duty to exercise reasonable care for their safety.*

The court noted, however, that:

> *It is the duty of the tenants or guests to exercise ordinary care for their own safety.*

The court upheld the jury's finding that the hotel was negligent in replacing its former wooden diving board with a "Duraflex" board of much greater elasticity, that projected divers farther into the pool. An expert testified that such a board at a three-meter height was unsafe for use by inexperienced divers into a hotel swimming pool. The court noted that there was nothing visually unsafe about the diving board, and that, "when a patron of … a hotel uses … facilities in the manner and method they were intended to be used, he does not assume the risk of injury, and is not chargeable with contributory negligence if he sustains an injury in so doing."

DUTIES OF A GUEST

There are some duties and obligations that are imposed on a guest as well, although they are far fewer and less difficult than those imposed on an innkeeper. The principal duty a guest owes to an innkeeper is to conduct himself or herself in a courteous and dignified manner at all times. This includes *not* throwing a loud and boisterous all-night party, damaging property, stealing towels and ashtrays, disturbing or intimidating other guests, and playing unsafely around the premises and fixtures of the hotel. Such irresponsible actions on the part of the guest go a long way toward relieving the innkeeper of responsibility for some of his duties (although it may put some of them into effect vis-a-vis *other*, well-behaved guests), and it may be used as a defense against actions brought against the innkeeper by such a guest.

Another major duty of a guest is to pay promptly and fully for the services provided by the innkeeper. The willful failure by a guest to do so is punishable as a crime in most jurisdictions. In some cases, the innkeeper has a lien against the baggage or other property of such a nonpaying guest. Execution of such lien should be handled with caution, however. Preventive Legal Care® tells us to make sure that all statutory legal formalities are complied with so that the hotel is not served with a countersuit under the theory that "the best defense is a good offense."

RIGHTS OF AN INNKEEPER

Once a guest has been received and duly registered by the innkeeper, the innkeeper himself obtains several important rights. Chief among these is the right to reasonably assign the guest to another room. This is because the guest's right is a license or privilege to occupy a room at the inn, rather than the right of a tenant to occupy a particular location for a particular time pursuant to a lease. This right may be limited, however, if the innkeeper and the guest have contracted in advance for a particular type of room, such as a suite or one with an ocean view. Then the innkeeper would have to provide similar or superior accommodations to avoid potential liability. At any rate, such a reassignment of rooms should not be done without good cause on the part of the innkeeper, and he should provide whatever assistance possible to minimize the inconvenience to the guest. If such a reassignment is contemplated, the innkeeper should always give the guest as much advance notice as possible, if possible prior to accepting the guest's registration.

Innkeepers also retain a limited right of entry into a guest's room. More than exists in a lease between landlord and tenant, innkeepers have a right of reasonable entry into a guest's room to provide for cleaning and maintenance. They also have a right of entry in the event of an emergency, such as fire or a broken water line in the room. Innkeepers can, and indeed must, enter to warn of outside danger, and they or their agents may enter to stop further damage to the room itself and to the possessions of the guest present in that room. Common sense is the controlling factor here, with courts looking to how a "reasonable innkeeper" would act in similar circumstances.

Another right vested in innkeepers is a right to eject. If they violate their rights and duties toward a guest, the guest may bring a cause of action in court. Conversely, if a guest violates his or her rights and duties toward the innkeeper, the innkeeper has a right to solve the problem by ejecting the guest. However, innkeepers must make sure that they have conducted a careful inquiry and that their grounds for ejecting the guest are solid, otherwise they will find themselves in court before they can turn around.

RIGHTS OF A GUEST

The rights of a guest are the reverse side of the coin that describes the duties of the innkeeper. In other words, a guest has a right to be received without discrimination, to a safe and adequate accommodation, and so on. The discrimination issue has provoked considerable litigation in the past. Freedom from discrimination is one of our basic civil rights and was made law in the Civil Rights Act of 1964.

> *(a) All persons shall be entitled to the full and equal enjoyment of the goods, services, facilities, privileges, advantages and accommodations of any place of public accommodation, as defined in this section, without discrimination or segregation on the ground of race, color, religion, or national origin.*
>
> *(b) Each of the following establishments which serves the public is a place of public accommodation within the meaning of this title if its operations affect commerce, or if discrimination or segregation by it is supported by State action:*
>
> *(1) any inn, hotel, motel, or other establishment which provides lodging to transient guests, other than an establishment located within a building which contains not more than five rooms for rent or hire and which is actually occupied by the proprietor of such establishment as his residence;*—Sec. 201, Title II, Civil Rights Act of 1964.

This law nullifies all local or state legislation that is inconsistent or in conflict with it. This issue has become almost academic since the United States Supreme Court upheld the Civil Rights Act of 1964, in rejecting several broad constitutional challenges.[3] In that case, a 216-room hotel on a major Georgia highway had a long-standing policy of refusing to rent rooms to blacks. The United States government challenged that policy and sought to prohibit the motel from its policy of racial discrimination.

---

3. *Heart of Atlanta Motel v. United States,* 379 U.S. 241 (1964).

The motel fought the court action, claiming that the federal Civil Rights Act had no applicability to a purely local motel operation. The court found that the motel advertised outside the state, and, being located near the intersection of two major highways, its policies had an effect upon *interstate* travel. Therefore, federal jurisdiction existed, and the federal Civil Rights Act properly applied to the motel's operations. Since the United States Supreme Court upheld the Civil Rights Act of 1964, this issue has become almost academic. It is a clear duty of those in the travel or lodging industry to provide accommodations on an equal basis without discrimination of any sort—with one exception in some jurisdictions: sex. However, given the nature of the times, that exception is now under attack and may well be gone within a few years.

Another important group of rights belonging to guests are their property rights. Under the common law, an innkeeper was completely responsible for the loss of a guest's property, unless the loss was caused by the traveler's own negligence or an act of God. The innkeeper thus became the insurer of the property of his guest. This strict standard has been modified by statute over the years, to limit the liability of innkeepers for their guests' property.

There are three ways in which the liability of innkeepers today may be limited: (1) by the rules of the inn or hotel; (2) by the use of contract disclaimers and disclosure notices; and (3) by statutory law. Innkeepers may develop and use reasonable rules to be followed by their guests. Once guests have notice of such a rule, they have a duty to obey it. If they do not, and loss results, they are negligent themselves and cannot hold the innkeeper liable. The innkeepers must make sure that the notice is understandable and clearly displayed, and may not use the hotel rules as a "dodge" behind which to escape genuine liability for their negligence. One such rule, very commonly seen, is the requirement that all valuables be deposited at the front desk for safekeeping, if the hotel is to assume limited responsibility for them and consequent limited liability for their loss.

This principle was affirmed by the U.S. District Court in a 1980 case where a couple completing a three-day stay at the St. Regis-Sheraton Hotel in New York checked their luggage with a bellhop for the afternoon.[4] They did not inform the hotel that one of the cases contained jewelry worth over $60,000, nor did they ask that it be placed in the hotel safe. When they returned that afternoon, the jewelry case was missing.

The court noted that the hotel had posted a notice informing guests that the hotel provided a safe for valuables, and notifying them that New York law provided that no hotel shall be liable for more than $100 for the loss or damage to luggage delivered to the hotel, unless the excess value is declared to the hotel and a written receipt is given to the guest stating the value of the lug-

---

4. *Salisbury v. St. Regis-Sheraton Hotel Corp.*, 490 F.Supp. 449 (S.D. N.Y. 1980).

gage checked. The court ruled that the Sheraton's liability was limited to $100.

While an innkeeper may set reasonable rules, many courts look with disfavor upon innkeepers' attempts to limit their liability by contractual disclaimers and releases. Many courts feel that such efforts by an innkeeper are invalid because they are contrary to public policy. The more common limitations of liability are those set by legislatures to keep up with the changing face of modern travel. Frequently, these laws create classes of property for guests. Among them are money and valuables, property in transit to and from the hotel, property destroyed by fire, and all other property of the guests.

A typical state statute allows innkeepers to keep a safe for the storage of their guests' valuables. Once a guest is given notice of this, failure to deposit such valuables with the hotel relieves the innkeeper of liability for their loss. Additionally, the law may create a statutory limit on how much can be deposited with the hotel, and the innkeeper does not have to accept any more than that limit for safekeeping. Also many state statutes have a limitation on the amount of liability an innkeeper may be held to at all. There may also be other limitations or excuses, such as requiring guests to make sure their doors are locked at all times. The notice of the house rules and statutory limitations of liability must be clearly posted, often using the wording of the statute itself. Usually it is posted on the door of every room, as well as in many public places.

Many states limit an innkeeper's liability for loss by fire, with one amount set if guests set a valuation at the time of checking their baggage with the innkeeper and another amount set by statute if they fail to state the value. These statutes require, however, that the innkeeper be without fault or negligence before his liability will be limited. If a fire occurs and the innkeeper is held to be at fault or negligent, then the statutory limitation of liability is lifted, and the guest may recover the actual value of the destroyed property. Contributory negligence of a guest may, however, limit or even eliminate the liability of the innkeeper.

Innkeepers are also liable for the loss or damage to the means of transportation of their guests. Based on principles that came down to us from horse and carriage days, innkeepers are generally strictly liable for the loss of a guest's automobile, motorcycle, or van, so long as the vehicle was "within the confines of the inn"—in other words, within the regular parking area of the hotel. Acts of God, such as natural disasters, were excused, and the guests could not be guilty of contributory negligence. For the innkeeper to be liable for damage to the vehicle, as opposed to loss, there usually has to be some showing of negligence on the part of the innkeeper. Many states have statutes allowing innkeepers to limit their liability with regard to guests' vehicles.

RESERVATIONS

Back when Chaucer's pilgrims were making their way to Canterbury, there were no such things as advance reservations, or prepaid bookings, or anything of the sort. One member of the party might gallop on to warn the innkeeper to get dinner started, but that was about it. The weary traveler just trusted to luck and hoped for the best. This "galloping reservationist" was the original "800" line operator and served its limited purpose.

With the increase in travel, coupled with improvements in communication, voyagers wanted a little more certainty in their travel arrangements. They wanted to know that they did indeed have a room for the night. They wanted to be able to stay at Inn A rather than Inn B. They wanted a room with a view instead of one in the back. They wanted a room with air conditioning, or a private bath, or whatever. What they didn't want was an unpleasant surprise at the end of a long and tiring day. So the advance reservation was born.

When travelers make a reservation or book a room at a hotel or inn, they automatically enter into a contract with the innkeeper. A reservation is a contract, pure and simple, and the legal requirements of a contract must be met. There must be a valid offer by the traveler to rent the room or by the innkeeper to let the room. The other party must accept. In other words, both sides must intend to form a binding agreement. The agreement must be for a legal purpose. The two parties must be competent to enter into such an agreement. Finally, there must be consideration—something of value given and received on both sides. This would include a promise by the traveler to take the room and a promise by the inn to provide it, with the terms and conditions sufficiently clear. When these requirements are met, as they usually are in the booking of a room, a contract has been entered into, and it is now the responsibility of both parties to meet their obligations.

This contract is a counterpart to the common law duty to receive all guests, discussed earlier in this chapter. A common law excuse not to receive, such as the inn is already full, would not apply as an excuse to the contract. If the innkeeper has entered into a contract to provide a room to a traveler, it is no defense that the inn is already full when that traveler arrives and seeks his or her room. There are few legal excuses for the nonperformance of a contract. They include impossibility, although what is an actual impossibility may not be a legal impossibility. If the inn is full, it might be an actual impossibility to give the guest a room, but that would not be a legal impossibility sufficient to excuse performance. Such legal impossibilities may include fire, war, natural disasters, and so forth.

If the inn requests that a reservation, or part of it, be paid for in advance, the guest has a duty to comply. This can be either in cash at the time of arrival, or by prepaid voucher or coupon, or credit card. Many hotels request the credit card number of guests when making reservations. This is good and common practice because it guarantees the hotel that its room will be paid for and assures travelers that the room will be waiting for them, no matter how late they might arrive.

Reservation or not, a traveler still has a duty to arrive in an acceptable or presentable condition. If not, the inn would be justified if it refused to accept the traveler, and the traveler would have breached the contract. If the inn could not relet the room for the night, the traveler could be both denied admittance and liable for the room charge. The inn also has a duty to accept late arrivals with a reservation. If the reservation is not going to be held beyond a certain time, this must be made extremely clear at the time the reservation is accepted. In other words, it must be made a condition of the contract. Nowadays, that problem is generally handled by guaranteeing payment of the first night by means of a credit card number, given to the inn at the time the reservation is made.

OVERBOOKING

One of the earliest and most famous examples of overbooking occurred during the reign of Caesar Augustus, on the 24th of December, at a small inn outside Bethlehem. Actually, there was no arranged contract and, while his most famous guests had to be accommodated in the stables, the innkeeper had really breached no legal duty. But what about travelers who have confirmed reservations, in some cases paid for, who arrive only to be told that "there's no room at the inn"?

Few things are so irritating to the traveler than being told his confirmed reservation is not being honored—and few things are likely to get a hotel or travel agent into court faster. Overbooking in hotels, as in airlines, is a fact of life. Frequently hotels, like airlines, that practice overbooking claim economic necessity for their actions. They claim that they have so many "no-shows" that they need to overbook to protect themselves financially. This may be true, but courts and juries are becoming increasingly more sympathetic to the outraged traveler, and are awarding bigger judgments when they find conscious disregard of consumers' rights. The majority rule is that a traveler is entitled to actual damages for breach of the contract itself. Traditionally punitive damages are not allowed for breach of contract, but today many jurisdictions are finding justification in other areas of the law to award damages for emotional distress, additional expenses suffered by the traveler, and other reasons. These damages are labeled punitive damages when the hotel or its employees act in an abusive or excessive manner toward the guests. They are labeled compensatory damages when there is no such outrageous or intentional behavior on the part of the hotel. Whatever they are called, such damages are being awarded more frequently and in greater amounts when a confirmed reservation is not honored by a hotel. This is especially true in situations where a hotel regularly overbooks and refers its overflow to a less expensive hotel, collects its full rate from the guest, pays off the less expensive hotel, and pockets the difference.

Credit card guarantees have come a long way in ending the overbooking syndrome. There the hotel is protected for at least one night, in that customers, by giving their credit card number, agree to pay for one night's lodging, even if they don't show up. That way, the room is there and paid for, whether the guest uses it or not.

Many states have passed or have pending legislation designed to reduce overbooking. Some of these statutes would allow the hotel to eject a guest who is staying beyond the agreed time, causing the overbooking problem. However, some of these statutes would even provide criminal penalties for instances of deliberate overbooking. So the trend is clear. Although hotel overbooking may be technically just a breach of contract, many jurisdictions are treating it more and more harshly and allowing greater sanctions against the hotel that would have formerly been just a simple breach of contract.

RESEARCH AND REVIEW

1. What is an innkeeper's basic duty of reception? Discuss.
2. Name and discuss other duties innkeepers have toward their guests.
3. What are the two main duties of guests toward their host innkeeper?
4. Describe an innkeeper's right of reassignment.
5. What is an innkeeper's right to eject?
6. What are the three ways in which the liability of innkeepers for the property of their guests may be limited?
7. What elements must be present in booking a room in order to create a valid and enforceable contract?
8. Describe the remedies a customer may have against a hotel if a confirmed reservation was not available as contracted for.

NOTES

CHAPTER 13

OVERDUE ACCOUNTS AND HOW TO COLLECT

Travel agents do not make their living through earned commissions—they make their living through earned commissions *collected.* Every business should have a definite plan on how to collect its accounts receivable.

Whenever a debt is owed to an agent by a supplier or a wholesaler or vice versa, the internal machinery set up by ASTA (the American Society of Travel Agents) and ARTA (the Association of Retail Travel Agents) may be used after initial requests for payment have been ignored. Before using these services, however, the agent must be certain that the claim is in fact justified. This would prevent the agent from being subject to defamation liability. Defamation is the making of a *false* statement about another that injures his or her (or its) reputation. Truth of the statement, therefore, is of utmost importance. Truth of the challenged statement is an absolute defense to an action for defamation. Various trade magazines provide "Letters to the Editor" columns which are the most effective means of giving the nonpaying or slow-paying property an "attitude adjustment" and at the same time informing others in the industry who the slow-commission payers are.

There are several precautionary steps that an agent may take to avoid a debt situation. First, the agent can check the customer's credit condition prior to accepting checks or granting any credit. The agent should remember that a travel agency is in the business of providing travel-related services and *not* in the business of financing travel-related services for other companies.

Second, try to avoid supplying services or incurring expenses before there is adequate assurance that the customer's check will clear or that his credit is good. If the purchase is for tickets and ground packages, try to deliver the vouchers *after* the passenger's check has been paid by the bank.

Third, maintain as much information as possible about the customer when giving credit of any kind or when accepting a check. This information may provide useful if future collection efforts are necessary. The basic information required should include:

1. The full name and address of the customer and spouse;
2. The full name and location of the employer;
3. The customer's car license number and driver's license number; and
4. The customer's social security number if he or she is willing to supply it.

The first step in collecting an overdue debt is to locate the debtor. The following sources may be useful in locating an address or at least a reference point for beginning your search for the absent debtor:

1. ***Previous Telephone Directories.*** Check old telephone directories to see whether an address is listed in the name of the debtor or the debtor's spouse. If you do not have access to or storage room for old phone books, the local library usually has a copy.

2. ***Certified Mail.*** If the absent debtor has left a new address with the post office, you may obtain the new address by sending a certified letter including a return card requesting the post office to advise the sender of the current address. Additionally, a forwarding address may be obtained by addressing a letter to the postmaster at the city, state, and ZIP code of the debtor's last known address and enclosing a check or money order for the service fee. You should check with your local post office to see what further procedures may be required.

3. ***The Department of Motor Vehicles.*** A written request to the Motor Vehicle Department in many states may result in information regarding the address of the debtor.

4. ***The Debtor's Employer.*** A call to the debtor's present or former employer may reveal the debtor's current address. However, you should be careful when contacting an employer and not discuss the debt with him. Keep your communication as brief as possible. Both federal and state laws permit only limited contact with the employer, do not permit you to reveal that the employee owes any debt, and limit you to one call, unless follow-up communication is needed to correct or clarify address information in a reasonable manner.

5. ***Voter Registration Records.*** Voter registration records are available for public viewing at city hall and would reveal the current address of the debtor, assuming he or she is a registered voter.

6. ***Employment Agencies***. If you know that the customer may have utilized employment agencies, you may contact these agencies to see if a current address is in their records. Again, you should only limit your inquiries to a request for information regarding the location of the debtor.

7. ***Real Estate Property Records***. Real estate property records at the Assessor's Office in the county the debtor owned property or had previously lived.

8. ***A Skip Tracing Firm or a Private Investigator.*** One of these may be a practical alternative when the amount of the debt justifies the added expense.

Once the debtor has been located, the next step is to send a demand letter for the amount owed. All demand letters must be sent in a closed envelope and addressed to the debtor. The travel agent should not send debt notices or requests for payments on postcards or in any manner that would indicate to another person that the addressee is being sought for bad debts.

As stated earlier, initial contacts should be attempted at the debtor's residence. As a last resort, employers, friends, or relatives of the debtor can be contacted discreetly.

The travel agent should be careful when threatening legal action against a debtor. It is important that the travel agent verify the validity of any claimed debt, since threatening legal action, especially one involving criminal investigation, can very well amount to extortion. *Extortion* is the type of crime that constitutes a felony and is punishable by a prison term of more than one year.

Demand letters may not be modeled after, or be confusingly similar to, official government forms. The letter should not be intended to make the person believe that the communication is from a court or government administrative office, which could be deemed to be a misdemeanor in some states. You do not want to give the debtor grounds to sue you with a cross-complaint, so be careful with your collection practices.

Although a creditor may be permitted to threaten a lawsuit, this privilege must not be abused. If repeated threats of lawsuit are made and no suit is brought, travel agents may be subject to lawsuits themselves for harassment and collection procedures. A general rule of thumb is to make no threat without taking action, if it is apparent that no money is forthcoming.

When communicating with the debtor, there are several general rules that the travel agent should apply. Contacts with the debtor should be made during reasonable hours of the day such as from 8AM to 9PM. The travel agent should avoid the use of abusive or intimidating language.

If the debtor promises to make payment after being contacted by the creditor, the creditor may make additional calls or communications to ensure that payment is being made. If the debtor has genuine questions regarding the validity of the debt, the creditor must respond in a timely fashion and address the issues raised by the inquiry. Whenever possible, communications with the debtor should be in writing, and the travel agent should request responses from the debtor in writing. This will eliminate any problems of proof if, in fact, the matter had to proceed to trial.

NEGOTIATION AND SETTLEMENT OF A DEBT

If the debtor owes money to several creditors, or is in serious financial difficulty, it may be worthwhile to "cut the losses" and try to reach a reasonable compromise of the debt. If all creditors insist on full payment, the debtor may very well declare bankruptcy and limit everyone's right to payment.

Litigation costs are expensive, and most collection agencies or a collection attorney are usually paid 50 percent of anything collected. Once the debt is assigned for collection to such agencies or attorneys, the collector is entitled to his percentage even if the debtor voluntarily pays the full amount directly to the creditor.

If a compromise amount is agreed upon, the creditor should have this agreement in writing. This will protect the creditor in the event the debtor does not honor the compromise amount. Under the rules of contract law, the debtor can then sue on the full amount due, once the compromise agreement has been breached. A new written agreement may also extend the time within which the law requires a lawsuit to be brought for collection of the debt. This is called the *statute of limitations.*

SMALL CLAIMS COURT ENFORCEMENT OF JUDGMENT

Most states have a special court called the small claims court to hear disputes over a relatively small amount.

This court has its own proceedings and jurisdiction, and you must check the local rules for the particular court to make sure which jurisdictional limits or amounts in controversy apply.

The dollar amount in controversy may vary from one jurisdiction to another. For example, the small claims court in California has jurisdiction over any dispute where the maximum in controversy is $5,000. If the amount in dispute is greater than $5,000, it is beyond the jurisdiction of the court, unless the plaintiff agrees to waive the excess amount.

In Cook County, Illinois, the amount in controversy cannot exceed $2,500. The Illinois courts also allow a jury trial if one is requested whereas most other states will not.

The amount in controversy for New York varies with each county within the state. In New York City the amount in controversy is limited to $1,500. Attorneys in New York may make appearances on behalf of individuals, whereas in California attorneys can only represent corporations in small claims court.

In Washington, D.C., the jurisdictional limit is $750. The District of Columbia small claims court also allows the presence of attorneys. Once a complaint is filed in small claims court, a trial date is set for the parties to appear. The proceedings are quite informal, and the judges usually conduct part of the questioning. Each party may bring witnesses to testify in support of his or her position. However, due to the time limitations involved, the court may restrict the number of witnesses for each party.

The main point to remember in presenting a case in small claims court is to be organized and concise. If there are supporting documents or writings, you should make copies for the opposing party, as well as for the court, so that papers will not have to be passed back and forth for review.

Once a judgment is rendered by the court, the winning party is called the *judgment creditor.* If you have sued for recovery of money that is due you, you have several tools available to collect or "enforce" your judgment. These legal tools include writs of attachment, garnishment of wages, share of sales, and orders of examination to determine what assets may exist and where they are located.

It should be noted that *enforcement of judgment* in each jurisdiction has its own set of rules and usually its own forms. The directions must be followed to the letter, and the courts are hesitant to allow any deviations.

In California and other states, one of the most useful tools in enforcement of a judgment in your favor is a procedure known as an *order of examination.* This procedure allows the judgment creditor the right to compel *judgment debtors* to be personally examined while under oath concerning the identity, amount, and location of their assets. If judgment debtors fail to appear at the scheduled examination, they may be subject to arrest for contempt of court. Once the debtor's assets have been identified and located, the judgment creditor should apply to the clerk of the court for what is known as a *writ of execution.* The writ of execution lists the amount of the judgment, any interest on the judgment that is accruing, and certain costs, such as service of process fees, sheriff's fees, etc., that may be recovered by the judgment creditor in his attempts to enforce the judgment.

In normal situations, contacting the local sheriff's office is probably the best way to enforce judgments. The sheriff's office will give instructions on the various fees for service of papers or levying against any assets that are held by the judgment debtor. The sheriff's office may also provide a written description of the various techniques and services available for enforcement of the judgment. To reiterate, you should check the local rules in your particular jurisdiction to determine what remedies are available in enforcing a judgment.

RESEARCH AND REVIEW

1. What precautionary steps should a travel agent take to avoid the creation of a debt to the agent?
2. List some of the basic information a travel agent should have about a customer prior to granting credit.
3. What steps can a travel agent take to locate a debtor?
4. Describe the steps a travel agent should follow to collect an overdue amount from a debtor, once that debtor has been located.
5. What actions should *not* be taken in an attempt to collect an overdue debt?
6. Describe the use of the small claims court in your state. What is the maximum amount you may sue for in your state's small claims court?

NOTES

CHAPTER 14

CORPORATE TRAVEL

For the travel agent who enjoys being under constant pressure from business executives, prefers mundane fare costing comparisons on the computer screen to multicolored brochures of exotic destinations, and doesn't mind working on the upper floors of an office building (where rents are lower and that discourage the possible "walk-in" customer from taking an hour of an agent's time explaining different destinations), I suggest the wonderful world of corporate travel.

Deregulation of the travel industry has caused increased confusion for both corporate and vacation travel agencies. However, it is the corporate travel agency that most bears the burden of dealing with the daily fare changes that were brought about when the former United States Civil Aeronautics Board (CAB) removed the requirement for prior publication and CAB approval of domestic air tariffs.

An interesting statistic I used in a *Travel Agent* magazine article was the number of domestic fare changes in a typical month, citing November 1987 when I was doing the research for the article. None of the travel industry experts, consultants, or teachers whom I questioned were within a few million of the actual figure. The answer to my question—how many domestic air changes were there in a month—ranged between 2,000 and 10,000. In reality, according to Airline Tariff Publishers, which compiles and relays these changes to various computer reservations systems, in November 1987 there were *seven million* air fare changes amounting to approximately 233,000 per day. Given that fact, note the risk to a corporate travel agent promising the "lowest possible fare." Honoring that promise can only be attempted using a multitude of reservations systems. Needless to say, the agent often fails to locate the lowest air fare for the same reason the customer would also—the fares are simply too numerous and change too frequently.

The main asset of a corporate travel agency is its ability to offer commercial businesses a variety of services that are not only cost-saving, but are designed to save and control costs for the agency's business customer. The types of services that corporate travel agencies would normally offer include the following:

1. ***Travel Management Services.*** These include monthly management summary reports; automated accounting systems; automated reservation boarding pass and ticketing machines on the customer's premises (satellite ticket printers or "STPs"), frequent ticket deliveries to the customer's office or, in some cases, lock boxes at the airports at which the customer's employees may pick up tickets.

Corporate agencies offer more than just reservations. They can act as consultants recommending less expensive travel patterns, alternate transportation, or even when a customer should reserve a car and driver instead of a rental car (for example, when numerous appointments need be made and traffic conditions are not conducive to driving a rental vehicle).

2. ***Corporate Protection Services.*** Various corporate agencies, through their fare checking computerization, will actually guarantee the customer receiving the lowest possible fare. This gives the customer the incentive of dealing with the agency for cost savings, and gives the agency a reason for making sure that the customer receives the lowest priced fare available, even though it may mean a smaller commission. These factors, of course, are taken into consideration when the corporate travel agent solicits the corporate business as its customer.

Certain corporate agencies are able to obtain preferred hotel rates through consortiums or franchises they belong to.

Because corporate travel agencies are normally equipped to handle large, million-dollar corporate accounts, they are, through their volume, sometimes able to "break space" when specific seats are needed on planes, to obtain late arrival guarantees at hotels, and to obtain special rental car rates that would normally be unavailable to a leisure travel agency.

Corporate travel agencies have recognized the trend among the nation's larger corporations to consolidate their travel purchases. Most have started their own trend to merge or consolidate into "mega-agencies" to compete for the larger corporate accounts.

In the half-million- to one-million-dollar range of corporate travel business, a Fortune 1000 survey of travel managers indicated that 85 percent of the companies or divisions in this price range utilized only one travel agency. In the one- to five-million-dollar sales range, approximately 72 percent used a single travel agency for their purchases.

"Your plane is waiting your arrival, Miss La Tour."

3. ***Individualized V.I.P. Services.*** Depending on the type of corporate customer and the hierarchy of travelers within that company, a large variety of specialized services are available through various corporate agencies.

Agencies, such as Hoffman Travel in Beverly Hills that cater to film and recording companies, might offer extensive greeting services to V.I.P. customers. These would include meeting the customers as a limousine drops them off, taking care of their baggage, escorting them to private airline clubs, and personally seeing that they get on the plane on time. Lower echelon customers would still have, through numerous corporate agencies subscribing to business services, a combination of 24-hour emergency reservations or problem-solving services, boarding passes, and special rates for hotels, cars, and other ground services.

4. ***Incentive Group and Conference Services.*** Certain corporate agencies may specialize in group and

incentive business. For example, such an agent might design or arrange a trip to a leisure destination (such as a one-week Hawaii package) for a group of corporate personnel who are either going to the destination to attend a meeting or are winners of the trip as part of an incentive sales program.

5. ***Corporate Support Services.*** Corporate agencies may wish to expand beyond ticket printers in the customer's location to actual "in-plant" (on-site) or "near-plant" agencies, which means moving personnel to or near the site of the corporate customer. Corporate travel agencies might assign certain specific agents to service a particular corporate account and then use other agency personnel to handle the leisure bookings that corporate personnel might request for their personal needs. Unfortunately, certain corporate travel agencies have tended to ignore leisure customers. Yet their efficient methods can benefit price-conscious consumers who want minimum service and maximum savings.

It is a very widespread practice for corporate accounts to request revenue sharing or rebates from the corporate agency. Rebating on domestic air fares is presently permitted, although international rebating (as of October 1994) is still illegal. Average rebates for smaller corporate agencies can be in the four percent to five percent range for air travel, three percent to four percent for car rentals utilizing special corporate rates, and six percent to seven percent on hotels, again utilizing reduced corporate hotel prices.

Because of the large profit that major corporate agencies can derive from their computer reservation systems, as well as the large overrides from various carriers, rebates much in excess of the four percent to five percent on air travel are becoming more and more prevalent.

Smaller corporate agencies often try to compete directly with the hundred-million-dollar-plus corporate agencies and find themselves giving away too much of their profits merely for the sake of obtaining volume in hopes that they, too, will obtain high airline override commissions. Chasing business in this way is at best a high-risk proposition.

SOLICITATION OF COMMERCIAL ACCOUNTS

The agent who decides to solicit small- to medium-sized corporate customers must similarly realize that there are numerous corporate agency competitors seeking those same accounts. No longer do we find the two-page letter from a corporate agency soliciting an account by attaching a brochure or a business card showing the agent's address. Elaborate cost-saving hints, account management, and accountability controls are now the effective means of presenting a proposal. "In-house" computerized graphics utilizing statistics obtained from the prospective corporate customer are common within the corporate travel industry and are as sophisticated as professional sales techniques in any field.

One rule recognized by virtually all corporate travel agencies is that without volume the agency will not receive special computer reservations system benefits, it will not receive significant carrier overrides, and, unless it is a member of a consortium or franchise service that supplies corporate benefits, it will not have the bargaining power (or "leverage") to obtain products at prices that its corporate customers will expect.

Many a large corporation that has decided to own its own agency for what it believes is more than mere control should first consider the risks involved if ticket stock is stolen from its premises and it is held responsible to the carriers for the full amount of the tickets. Preventive Legal Care® normally suggests the ownership be left in the hands of the travel professionals.

Agents are sometimes asked to write fares such as "Government Fares for Subcontractors," "Hidden City" tickets, "Back to Back" tickets or manipulate advance purchase requirements. If these practices are engaged in by your corporate travel agents, the following disclosure notice should be given to the corporate client:

NOTICE

> The enclosed represents the itinerary requested. Some airlines dispute agency tariff interpretations. If we are debited by the carrier on this requested itinerary the purchaser agrees to reimburse our agency for costs and expenses imposed by carrier(s) and paid by the agency. All use of such tickets is done at travelers' risk and agency shall not be responsible for any consequences that may result.

RESEARCH AND REVIEW

1. What differentiates the corporate agency from the leisure travel agency?
2. What additional corporate services could you offer a prospective corporate customer if you were managing a corporate travel agency?
3. Why is gross volume so important to the corporate travel agency?

NOTES

APPENDIX

SAMPLE SERVICE CHARGE AGREEMENT

I, (CUSTOMER'S NAME), authorize Mr./Mrs. (AGENT'S NAME) of (AGENCY NAME), (CITY, STATE, ZIP) to proceed with all my travel arrangements, as of today, (DATE), and by so authorizing, I agree to pay for any/all expenses incurred by and/or services rendered by (AGENCY NAME) over and above the price of airline/cruise tickets and ground tours and accommodations including but not limited to:

1. Telephone, telex and other correspondence costs;
2. Planning detailed "personalized" itineraries:
3. Obtaining "exclusive" accommodations or entry to "special events" and "extras."

If above costs exceed $______________, I, (CUSTOMER'S NAME), must be so informed before additional agency costs are accrued on my behalf.

Unless and until authorized by law, no service charge will be made for making or cancelling airline reservations or issuing/changing tickets for air transportation.*

I further understand and agree that a cancellation fee of $______________ will be charged if reservations made by this agency upon my request are cancelled.

If any action at law or in equity is necessary to enforce or interpret the terms of this agreement, the prevailing party shall be entitled to reasonable attorney's fees, costs, and necessary disbursements in addition to any other relief to which he/she may be entitled.

(AGENCY NAME) (DATE)

By: (AGENT'S SIGNATURE)

By: (CUSTOMER'S SIGNATURE)

(NUMBER AND STREET)

(CITY, STATE, ZIP)

(TELEPHONE/BUS)

(TELEPHONE/HOME)

** The preceding "Service Charge" Agreement has been prepared as an example only. It should not be taken as legal or professional advice. Anyone intending to use this Agreement as a form should modify its language or substitute other provisions where, as will always be the case, the circumstances of a particular relationship require. It is suggested that every travel agent contact his or her travel attorney to determine what particular or additional provisions apply to an individual Agreement.*

TRAVEL AGENCY GENERAL PARTNERSHIP CONTRACT

This Partnership Agreement is entered into and effective as of____________________, 19___ , by_______________ and _______________ ("The Partners").

The Partners desire to form a General Partnership under the laws of the State of ___________ for the purpose of operating a retail travel agency, accredited by the Airlines Reporting Corporation (ARC) and the International Airline Travel Agent Network (IATAN) and (CRUISE) Conference(s), and on the terms and conditions stated in this Agreement.

The parties to this Agreement agree to become Partners and form a General Partnership under the laws of the State of ____________________, and therefore agree as follows:

1. The name of the Partnership shall be (AGENCY NAME) (INCLUDE ANY DBA)

2. The Partnership's principal place of business shall be at__________(AGENCY ADDRESS)__ in______________County, __________________. The principal place of business may be changed from time to time and other places of business may be established by actions taken in accordance with the provisions of this Agreement that govern management of the Partnership's business and affairs.

3. The Partnership shall begin as of the date of this Agreement and shall continue until dissolved by mutual agreement by all of the Partners or under the provisions of dissolution and winding

up in this Agreement, in accordance with applicable State law provisions.

4. The purposes of the Partnership are to engage in the business of providing travel services to the general public, and to do all things related to, incidental to, or in furtherance of that business, including acquiring and retaining the requisite carrier and cruise conference appointments.

5. The Partnership's initial capital shall consist of cash to be contributed by the Partners in the following amounts:

Name	Amount
____________________	$____________________
____________________	$____________________
____________________	$____________________

[The minimum initial and constant capitalization requirement of IATAN should be considered and agreed to by the Partners.]

Each Partner's contribution shall be paid in full within______________ (__) days after the date of this Agreement.

6. If any Partner fails to pay or convey his/her initial contribution to the Partnership's capital at the time and in the form and amount required by this Agreement, the Partnership shall immediately dissolve, and each Partner who has paid or conveyed all or any portion of his/her initial contribution to the Partnership's capital shall be entitled to a return of the funds and properties he/she contributed.

7. Whenever it is determined by the written Agreement of Partners holding a majority in capital interest of the Partnership that its capital is or is presently likely to become insufficient for the conduct of its business, those Partners may, by written notice to all Partners, call for additional contributions to the capital. These contributions shall be payable in cash no later than the date specified in the notice or no sooner than five (5) days after the notice is given. Each Partner shall be liable to the Partnership for his/her share of the aggregate contributions duly called for under this paragraph. Each Partner's share shall be in proportion to a share of the partnership profits, but no Partner shall be required in the event of such call to contribute more than __________ ($__________).

8. No Partner may make any voluntary contribution of capital to the Partnership without the consent of all the Partners.

9. No Partner may withdraw capital from the Partnership without consent of all the Partners.

10. No Partner shall be entitled to receive any interest on his/her capital contribution, except that, if he/she is entitled to repayment of his/her contribution, he/she shall also be entitled to interest on it at the rate of ____________ percent (___%) per annum, from the date payment should have been made.

11. The Partnership's profits and losses shall be shared among the Partners as follows:

Name	Percentage
______________________	________________%
______________________	________________%
______________________	________________%

12. Within ________ (___) days after the end of each fiscal year of the Partnership, there shall be distributed in cash to the Partners, in proportion to their respective shares in the Partnership's profits, amounts equal to the Partnership's net profit for that fiscal year computed under this Agreement.

13. The aggregate amount distributed to the Partners from the Partnership's profits shall not, however, exceed the amount of cash available for distribution, taking into account the Partnership's reasonable working capital needs as determined by a majority in capital interest of the Partners.

14. The fiscal year of the Partnership shall be one (1) ending on __________ of each year.

15. The Partnership's books shall be kept on the (CASH OR ACCRUAL) basis.

16. The Partnership's net profit or net loss for each fiscal year shall be determined as soon as practicable after the close of that fiscal year in accordance with the accounting principles employed in the preparation of the Federal Income Tax Return filed by the Partnership for that year, but without any special provisions for tax-exempt or partially tax-exempt income.

17. Proper and complete books of account of the travel agency shall be kept at the Partnership's principal place of business and shall be open to

inspection by any of the Partners or their accredited representatives at any reasonable time during business hours. The accounting records shall be maintained in accordance with generally accepted bookkeeping practices for travel agencies, including the weekly sales reports required by the air carrier conferences.

18. Each Partner shall participate in the control, management, direction, and business of the Partnership. In exercising this control, management, and direction, each Partner's vote shall be in proportion to his/her interest in the Partnership's profits.

[ALTERNATIVE IF A MANAGING PARTNER IS TO BE USED]

18a. The Managing Partner shall be ______________. He/She shall have control of the business of the Partnership and assume direction of its business operations. He/She shall consult and confer as far as practicable with the nonmanaging Partners, but the power of decision shall be vested in him/her. His/Her powers and duties shall include control over the Partnership's books and records and hiring any independent Certified Public Accountant he/she deems necessary for this purpose.

Except as otherwise expressly provided in this Agreement, all things to be done by the Partnership shall be done under the Managing Partner's control and supervision. The Managing Partner shall be entitled to reimbursement monthly, on the submission of an itemized account, of any sums he/she shall have expended for the benefit of the Partnership's business. On the Managing Partner's death, resignation, or other disability, a successor Managing Partner of the agency shall be selected by a majority in capital interest of the Partners. Upon any of these occurrences, appropriate notification of a Change of Ownership shall be filed immediately with the Airlines Reporting Corporation, International Airline Travel Agent Network, and ___(CRUISE)_____ Conference(s).

19. The following acts may be done only with the consent of a majority in capital interest of the Partners:

a. Borrowing money in the Partnership's name;
b. Transferring income or hypothecating, compromising, or releasing any Partnership claim, except on payment in full;
c. Selling, leasing, or hypothecating any Partnership property or entering into any contract for any such purpose, other than in the ordinary course of the Partnership's business;
d. Knowingly suffering or causing anything to be done whereby a Partnership property may be seized or attached or taken in execution, or its ownership or possession otherwise endangered.

20. All Partnership funds shall be deposited in the Partnership's name and shall be subject to withdrawal only on the signatures of at least ________ (____) Partners.

[ALTERNATIVE IF A MANAGING PARTNER IS TO BE USED]

20a.All Partnership funds shall be deposited in the Partnership's name and shall be subject to withdrawal only on the signature of the Managing Partner.

21. Partnership funds referred to in 20. (or 20a.) are separate and distinct from the travel agency funds to be deposited in the ARC Area Settlement Plan Account. The ARC Area Settlement Plan Account is under control of the "qualifying manager" so listed on applications submitted to ARC and IATAN. The "qualifying manager" may be a Managing Partner or an employee of the Partnership so designated with authority to manage the daily operation of the travel agency for the Partners.

If and when there is a change in the person designated as "qualifying manager" of the agency, the Partners shall immediately notify ARC and IATAN of said change, with particulars showing that the new person is qualified under current rules.

22. Any Partner may be engaged in one or more businesses, other than the business of the Partnership, but only to the extent that this activity does not compete or materially interfere with the business of the Partnership and does not conflict with the obligations of that Partner under this Agreement. Neither the Partnership nor any other Partner shall have any right to any income or profit

derived by a Partner from any business activity permitted under this section.

23. Each Partner shall be entitled to a monthly salary as follows:

Name	Amount
____________________	$____________________
____________________	$____________________
____________________	$____________________

or, such other amounts that from time to time may be determined by the unanimous written consent or agreement of all the Partners. These salaries shall be treated as Partnership expenses in determining its profits or losses.

24. Any assignment or hypothecation by a Partner of his/her interest in the Partnership shall terminate his/her rights to receive a salary from the Partnership.

25. The Partnership shall dissolve and terminate on any Partner's death, permanent physical or mental disability, or voluntary withdrawal from the Partnership.

[ALTERNATIVE PROVIDING FOR CONTINUATION OF BUSINESS]

25a. The Partnership shall not dissolve or terminate on any Partner's death, permanent physical or mental disability or voluntary withdrawal from the Partnership if, within________________ (____) days after the Partnership has received notice of the Partner's death, disability, or desire to withdraw, it elects to purchase his/her interest.

If the Partnership so elects, it may purchase that interest and thereafter continue and it shall not wind up its affairs or liquidate because of the death, disability or withdrawal. The vote of Partners holding a majority in capital interest in the Partnership (excluding the interest of the deceased, disabled, or withdrawing Partner) shall be sufficient to make the election to purchase. The price to be paid for the interest of the deceased, disabled, or withdrawing Partner shall be equalled to the value of that interest as determined under this Agreement.

26. In the event of the death, withdrawal, expulsion or bankruptcy of any Partner, the remaining Partners are responsible to notify ARC and IATAN and other Conferences immediately of the Change of Ownership status and comply with the conferences' current Resolutions covering the respective Change of Ownership approval procedure.

27. Following dissolution of the Partnership on the voluntary withdrawal of any Partner, the withdrawn Partner shall not carry on a business similar to the business of the Partnership within the (COUNTIES OR CITIES)_____ for a period of________________ (___) years.

28. A Partner may be expelled from the Partnership by the vote of the other Partners holding at least__________ percent (___%) in capital interest of the Partnership (excluding the interest of the Partner to be expelled) if, by this vote, it is determined in the sole discretion of those Partners that the Partner to be expelled has materially

breached or is unable to perform his/her material obligation under this Agreement or that the continued association of that Partner with the Partnership is detrimental to the best interest of the Partnership's business.

Expulsion shall become effective when written notice of expulsion is served on the expelled Partner. When expulsion becomes effective, the expelled Partner's rights to participate in the Partnership's profits and to draw a salary, and his/her other rights, powers, and authority as a Partner of the Partnership shall terminate.

If, as of the effective date of expulsion:

a. His/Her share of the Partnership's undistributed profits for the current fiscal year;
b. The credit balance in his/her credit account; and
c. Any Partnership indebtedness to him/her, reduced by:
    (1) any indebtedness of the expelled Partner to the Partnership; and
    (2) his/her drawings for the current fiscal year,

is a credit balance, that balance shall be a debt due on demand owed to the expelled Partner by the Partnership. If that balance is a debit balance it shall be a debt due on demand owed to the Partnership by the Partner.

The remaining Partners must file appropriate notifications with the carrier and cruise conferences of the Change of Ownership status of the travel agency and comply with current Resolutions affecting such a change.

29. If (a) any Partner files a voluntary petition in bankruptcy, is adjudicated bankrupt, becomes insolvent, makes an assignment for the benefit of creditors, or applies for or consents to the appointment of a receiver or trustee with respect to any substantial part of his/her assets, or if (b) a receiver or trustee is appointed or an attachment or execution levied with respect to any substantial part of any Partner's assets and the appointment is not vacated or the attachment of execution is not released within ____________ (__) days, or if (c) a charging order is issued against any Partner's interest in the Partnership and is not released or satisfied within _____________ (__) days, that Partner shall then cease to be a Partner and shall have no interest in common with the remaining Partners in the Partnership or its properties. From the date of that event, he/she shall be considered in equity as a vendor to the Partnership of his/her share of the Partnership's assets at a price equal to the credit balance in his/her capital account at that date, as increased by his/her share of any Partnership net profit, and decreased by his/her share of any Partnership net loss, not yet reflected in his/her capital account. That amount shall be considered a debt due on demand owed by the Partnership to that Partner or his/her assignee or trustee, and all necessary deeds and documents shall be executed for vesting of the Partner's share and the Partnership.

30. If any Partner receives an offer, whether or not solicited by him/her from a person not then a Partner to purchase all or any portion of his/her

interest in the Partnership, and if the Partner receiving the offer is willing to accept it, he/she shall give written notice of the amount and terms of the offer, the identity of the proposed transferee, and his/her willingness to accept the offer of each of the other Partners. The other Partners shall have the option, within ____________ (__) days after that notice is given, to purchase the designated interest or the designated portion of the interest of the Partner giving notice on the same terms as those contained in the offer. The other Partners may exercise this option jointly or individually. If more than one (1) Partner exercises the option individually, the Partner giving notice may choose whose exercise of the option he/she shall accept.

31. Except as otherwise provided, the value of a Partner's interest in the Partnership for the purposes of this Agreement shall be determined by appraisal as follows:

Within ____________ (__) days after the occurrence requiring appraisal or, in the case of a Partner's death or legal disability, within__________ (__) days after the appointment of the personal representative, the Partnership and the Partner whose interest is to be appraised, or his/her personal representative either:

a. Shall jointly appoint an appraiser with travel agency appraisal experience for this purpose; or
b. Failing this joint action, each shall separately designate an experienced travel agency appraiser and, within ______________ (__)

days after their appointment, the two (2) designated appraisers shall jointly designate a third (3rd) similarly qualified appraiser.

The failure of either the Partnership, or the Partner whose interest is being appraised, or his/her personal representative to appoint an appraiser, within the time allowed shall be deemed equivalent to appointing the appraiser selected by the other party. No person shall be appointed or designated an appraiser unless he/she is familiar with the travel agency business and operation of such business within the carrier and cruise conference accreditation system.

If, within ______________ (___) days after the appointment of all appraisers, a majority of the appraisers concur on the value of the interest being appraised, that appraisal shall be binding as conclusive. If a majority of the appraisers do not concur within that period, the determination of the appraiser whose appraisal is neither highest nor lowest shall be binding and conclusive. The Partnership and the Partner whose interest is to be appraised, or his/her estate or successors, shall share the appraisal expenses equally if there is a single appraiser. If 31(b) is utilized, each party shall be responsible for the expenses and costs of the appraiser each so chooses, and additionally, share his/her proportionate share of the third appraiser.

32. Except as otherwise provided, whenever the Partnership is obligated, or having the right to do so, chooses to purchase a Partner's interest, it shall pay for the interest in cash

within __________ (__) days after the date in which the Partnership's obligation to pay has become fixed.

33. Except as otherwise provided, the continuing Partnership shall pay, as they mature, all Partnership obligations and liabilities that exist on the effective date of termination and shall hold the terminating Partner harmless from any acts or claims arising, or alleged to arise from those obligations or from liabilities accruing after that date.

34. On any dissolution of the Partnership under this Agreement or applicable law, except as otherwise provided in this Agreement, the continuing operation of the Partnership's business shall be confined to those activities reasonably necessary to wind up the Partnership affairs, discharge its obligations, and preserve and distribute its assets. If the Partnership dissolves the travel agency business, notification of such dissolution must be given to carrier and cruise conferences, to affect appropriate discharge of any agency obligations.

35. Each Partner shall indemnify and hold harmless the Partnership and each of the Partners from any and all expenses and liabilities resulting from or arising out of any negligence or misconduct on his/her part to the extent that the amount exceeds the applicable insurance carried by the Partnership.

36. This Agreement may be amended at any time and from time to time, but any amendment must be in writing and signed by each person who is then a Partner.

37. Any written notice to any of the Partners required or permitted under this Agreement shall be deemed to have been duly given on the date of service if served personally on the party to whom notice is to be given, or on the third (3rd) day after mailing, if mailed to the party to whom notice is to be given, by first-class or air mail, certified, postage prepaid, and addressed to the addressee at the address directly opposite below, or at the most recent address, specified by written notice, given to the sender by the addressee under this provision. Notices to the Partnership shall be similarly given and addressed to it at its principal place of business:

____

NAME

____

STREET ADDRESS

____

CITY, STATE, ZIP

38. This Agreement is executed and intended to be performed in the State of ____________, and the laws of that State shall govern its interpretation and effect.

39. This Agreement shall be binding on and inure to the benefit of the respective successors, assigns and personal representatives of the parties, except to the extent of any contrary provision in this Agreement.

40. Any controversy or claim arising out of, or related to, this Agreement, or the making, performance, or interpretation thereof, shall be settled by arbitration in (CITY AND STATE)____________ in accordance with the rules of the American Arbitra-

tion Association then existing, and judgment on the arbitration award may be entered in any Court having jurisdiction over the subject matter of the controversy.

41. If any term, provision, covenant or condition of this Agreement is held by a Court of competent jurisdiction to be invalid, void, or unenforceable, the rest of the Agreement shall remain in full force and effect and shall in no way be effected, impaired or invalidated.

42. This instrument contains the entire agreement of the parties relating to the rights granted and obligations assumed in this instrument. Any oral representations or modifications concerning this instrument shall be of no force or effect unless contained in a subsequent written modification signed by the party to be charged.

IN WITNESS WHEREOF, the Partners have executed this Agreement as of the date first shown above.

______________________ residing at ___________

____

______________________ residing at ___________

____

______________________ residing at ___________

The preceding Travel Agency General Partnership Agreement has been prepared as an example only. It does not constitute legal or professional advice. Anyone intending to use this Agreement should modify the language or substitute other provisions where, as will always be the case, the circumstances of a particular transaction require. It is suggested that every agent contact his/her attorney to determine what particular or additional contract provisions apply to an individual transaction.

INDEX

A

B

C

D

E

F

G

H

I

J

K

L

M

NOTES

NOTES

NOTES